A Righteous Cause

THE LIFE OF WILLIAM JENNINGS BRYAN

*The humblest citizen in all the land,
when clad in the armor of a righteous cause,
is stronger than all the hosts of error.*
WILLAM JENNINGS BRYAN, 1896

Robert W. Cherny

A Righteous Cause

THE LIFE OF
WILLIAM JENNINGS BRYAN

Edited by Oscar Handlin

LITTLE, BROWN AND COMPANY • BOSTON • TORONTO

Library of Congress Cataloging in Publication Data

Cherny, Robert W.
  A righteous cause.

  (The Library of American biography)
  Bibliography: p.
  1. Bryan, William Jennings, 1860–1925. 2. Statesmen—
United States—Biography. 3. United States—Politics and
government—1865–1933. I. Handlin, Oscar, 1915–
II. Title. III. Series.
E664.B87C47 1984   973.91′092′4 [B]   84-19434
ISBN 0-316-13856-8

Copyright © 1985 by Robert W. Cherny

Library of Congress Catalog Card No. 84-19434

ISBN 0-316-13854-1

ALP

Published simultaneously in Canada
by Little, Brown & Company (Canada) Limited

Printed in the United States of America

Produced by Ron Newcomer & Associates

to my parents

Editor's Preface

EMPTINESS WAS THE MAGNET that drew Americans westward after the Civil War. Space challenged the imagination of farmers hemmed in at home, and expanding markets for food in the growing cities of the east and of Europe promised limitless opportunities for gain. Meanwhile transatlantic migration added to the population of the United States and stimulated the westward thrust. Thousands of enterprising families looked to the open acres of the great plains for the sites of homesteads on which they could earn fortunes.

In their train came a crowd of other settlers, also seeking western fulfillment of their aspirations. Little towns appeared in which merchants and professional people served the needs of the surrounding countryside. Among them were physicians, ministers, and teachers, but above all lawyers who manned the system of justice and who acted as political spokesmen for other settlers. A curious relationship developed between the lawyers in town and the rural population. Rarely was a farmer himself in the position to take time off to serve in the legislature or to deal with the complexities of ever more formal law. Increasingly the attorney served as intermediary in these matters. Book learning helped in the cases before courts, and oratory was the instrument of assertion in legislatures and political contests.

All too often, extravagant hopes doomed the settlers to disappointment. They had come not simply to get by, but to satisfy dreams of plenty: they overextended themselves in speculative debt, and frequently buried their hopes with adverse turns of the economic tide. Their grievances were soil fertile for protest. Unwilling to blame themselves or their excessive expectations, they ascribed their failure to the railroads, the grain elevators, or the banks and turned to government to correct deficiencies in the social system. Often these protests focused on monetary reforms. But in a larger sense they raised questions about the profound economic and social changes then transforming the United States.

William Jennings Bryan grew up in this setting. Oratorical power in 1896 won him the Democratic presidential nomination at the age of thirty-six, and he long remained a dominant figure in the western party. Although he failed in his three tries for the presidency, his rhetoric was important in expressing the wishes of an immense following. He played an important part in the election of Woodrow Wilson, whom he served as Secretary of State. But agrarian hopes by then were anachronistic. The war crushed them. Bryan spent the final years of his life in a futile effort to cling to the past, espousing prohibition and fundamentalism. These important developments are the subject of Professor Cherny's careful biography, which traces both the man and his background.

OSCAR HANDLIN

Acknowledgments

I am grateful to many people who provided assistance and encouragement in the preparation of this manuscript. I owe thanks to the staffs of the libraries where I did research for this work: the Library of Congress, especially the Manuscript Division and Photographic Division; the Nebraska State Historical Society, especially the State Archives and the Photograph Room; the Occidental College Library, Special Collections; Love Library, University of Nebraska; Leonard Library, San Fransisco State University; Doe Library, University of California, Berkeley; and the San Francisco Public Library. Oscar Handlin provided helpful comments on the style of the manuscript and made important suggestions regarding substance. Special thanks are due to two of the leading Bryan scholars in the nation, Paolo E. Coletta and Paul W. Glad, who gave generously of their time to read and comment on the manuscript. Paul Glad also provided a copy of the letter by Edgar Lee Masters quoted in the concluding chapter. Several of my colleagues at San Francisco State have read the manuscript, in part or whole, and I owe them a debt for their comments on both style and substance: Jerald Combs, James V. Compton, William Issel, Phil B. Johnson, and Frances Keller. Thanks also must go to Robert Rogers, Dean of Graduate Studies and Research at San Francisco State, for his assistance in locating funds to help with my trip to Washington to use materials in the Library of Congress. All errors are, of course, my own.

To improve readability, I have corrected errors of spelling and grammar where they occur in source materials.

ROBERT W. CHERNY

Contents

A Righteous Cause

THE LIFE OF WILLIAM JENNINGS BRYAN

I

Youth of a Crusader

IN 1887, THE FIRST DAY of October had a double significance for twenty-seven-year old William Jennings Bryan. Three years before, he and Mary Baird had pronounced their wedding vows. Now, on his third wedding anniversary, the tall, black-haired lawyer stepped down from a train in Lincoln, Nebraska, the city he and Mary had chosen as their future home. Mary and the family remained in Illinois while Will came ahead to find a house and to begin a new law practice with Adolphus Talbot, a friend from law school.

It must have seemed that Will brought very little with him to start a new life. He had his clothes and his law books, to be sure, but little more of a material nature. In his head and his heart, however, he carried a set of values, beliefs, attitudes, and expectations bred during his childhood and youth. Bryan had grown up in the America of farms and small towns, of religious revivals and church socials, of Civil War and its aftermath. To know what he carried with him that day in October, it is necessary to begin in Salem, Illinois, where Bryan was born on March 19, 1860.

Salem, county seat of Marion County, drew its economic life from agriculture. In 1870, only two towns in the county held more than a thousand residents; four out of five county residents lived outside those two towns. A majority of the county's families earned their livelihood by tilling the soil. Most who did not farm ran small businesses, selling goods

1

William Jennings Bryan, age 21, the year he graduated from Illinois College and entered Union College of Law. (Photograph courtesy of the Nebraska State Historical Society.)

and services to the farmers and to each other. In 1870, the town of Salem counted 342 people with identifiable occupations other than farmer or farm laborer. About a hundred worked as artisans: carpenters, saddle and harness makers, shoemakers, butchers, bakers, blacksmiths, milliners. Most artisans worked in their own shops, usually without assistance except from family members. Another seventy provided personal services, half as domestic servants, most of the others as launderers, saloonkeepers, hotelkeepers, and barbers. The town counted nearly equal numbers of professionals—teachers, physicians, and lawyers—and of merchants, bankers, brokers, or agents. As county seat, Salem claimed nearly two dozen government officials, most of them serving the town and county. Manufacturing was limited and small in scale; members of the community purchased the flour and lumber produced by Salem's three mills. They also bought most of the plows, wagons, and carriages made in Salem's one manufacturing shop. The mills each employed four to six workers; the shop occasionally hired as many as eleven. Only one adult Salemite in five worked for wages, most of them as domestic servants, day laborers, teachers, or store clerks. Agriculture controlled the economic destiny of the entire population. If crops were good and prices steady, the merchants, artisans, proprietors, and professionals of Salem prospered along with the farmers. In his most famous speech, Bryan was to proclaim, "destroy our farms and the grass will grow in the streets of every city in the country." His dictum unquestionably held true for Salem and thousands of other towns like it.

In the year of Willy's sixth birthday, his family moved from the house where he had been born to a new home on a farm just outside Salem. Willy's father, Silas Bryan, a lawyer and judge of the circuit court, believed in hard work, in "the sweat of the face in agricultural pursuits." Judge Bryan's farm—purchased with income from bar and bench—was one of the largest in the county. There Willy grew up, bearing his full share of farm chores: chopping wood, caring for livestock, milking cows, haying. He recalled it later as "drudgery" but acknowledged that it was probably responsible for his physical strength.

Farm work taxed the strength of most farmers, for much of it was based on human muscle power. Silas Bryan, more country gentleman than serious farmer, sometimes paid laborers to help with the most difficult tasks, especially in the summer. A farmer's work day began at sunrise—sometimes before—and lasted until sunset. Chores such as feeding and watering stock, milking, and gathering eggs demanded daily attention, usually at the same time. Other work varied according to the seasons. Every family member had chores, but everyone pitched in when an extra hand was needed; farm children might come to school exhausted after spending much of the night with farrowing or calving. A few important labor-saving innovations, notably the reaper, had appeared before the Civil War, but in 1866, when Silas moved his family to the farm, farmers worked in much the same way as those of a century before.

Families in Salem or on nearby farms knew each other, at least by reputation. Virtually all relationships were between people who knew each other in multiple social and economic roles. Salem township—Salem village and the rural areas a few miles in each direction, forming a square six miles on each side—contained 2,041 people in 1870, half of them children. The average home held nearly six people, usually related by kinship; a number included a boarder or a live-in servant. Frequently in face-to-face contact at church functions, lodge meetings, and in stores and shops, people could keep few secrets. The community knew who regularly attended Sunday school and church, and knew as well who regularly patronized saloons. People who violated dominant standards risked being labled as "not of the better sort."

Willy Bryan's family occupied a secure place among "the better sort." His father Silas served both as circuit court judge and as deacon of the Baptist church. Willy's mother,

Mariah, came from the Jennings family, one of the oldest in the county, and she took an active part in the Methodist church for many years before joining her husband's denomination. Silas Bryan was one of the most important men in town. In 1870 he owned $18,000 worth of real and personal property, a sum which put him sixth in the township. A history published in 1881 described him as one of five Salem residents to have achieved "state or national reputations." His judicial circuit included a half-dozen counties; travel often kept him away from home for days at a time. Well-known in a number of communities, Silas Bryan came within a few votes of being elected to the House of Representatives in 1872.

Most residents of Salem and other small towns led a more isolated life than Silas Bryan. Travel was usually limited to the distance a horse could travel in a day. A farmer's once-a-year trip to sell grain necessitated extensive preparations— loading the wagon the night before, rising before sunrise, traveling until noon, selling the grain, making a few purchases, then returning home long past sunset. Some family members stayed home to care for the stock and milk the cows, tasks that could not be ignored even for a day.

Though most small town residents traveled little beyond the boundaries of their own communities, news from the outside world was easily available. Salem had several weekly newspapers, most with a strong commitment to one of the major political parties. Willy's father undoubtedly subscribed to the *Salem Advocate,* the staunch voice of the local Democratic party. None in a series of weekly Republican papers was very successful; other short-lived papers espoused the Greenback party or the Baptist church. A half-dozen other weekly papers were printed in the other villages and towns of Marion County. Silas Bryan's family may also have taken one of the national weeklies or monthlies; magazines such as *Atlantic Monthly, Harper's Monthly,* or *Lippincott's* treated their readers to a wide variety of articles, everything from essays on Charles Dickens to accounts of spiritualism. Farm journals also flourished, devoted to the improvement of agriculture, but often also including fiction and travel accounts.

Although residents of Salem could read about slums in London and explorations in Africa, the outside world rarely touched them directly. Salem lived a relatively self-sufficient economic and political life. Members of the community owned and operated every business in Salem except the railroad and the telegraph office. Salem's economy could not claim immunity from national patterns of prosperity and depression, but its small manufacturing concerns produced for a local market and felt less susceptibility to variations in demand than the New England mills that produced cloth, clocks, and other items for Salem stores. When wheat and corn prices fell, however, so did patronage at the shops and stores along Main Street. Outside political forces seldom intruded on the lives of Salem residents. Local government touched Salem residents most directly, providing schools and roads and settling disputes over land ownership. State and federal governments were both remote and seldom seen. When Willy was a toddler, the Civil War touched every household in the nation. With that exception, the federal government did little to affect most citizens—it neither taxed them, regulated their enterprises, nor defined their social relationships.

The self-sufficiency of most village households mirrored the autonomy of the village. Salem houses usually sat in large yards, with lawn and maple trees in the front and space in the back for fruit trees, a large vegetable garden, a poultry yard, a barn if the family kept a cow or horses, and perhaps a pigpen. Nearly all families, whether on the farm or in town, produced much of their food, resorting to the grocery for sugar, coffee, spices and specialty items. The women of the house, aided perhaps by a hired seamstress, also produced clothing for the children and women. (In 1870, Salem counted only six grocers and five butchers, but fourteen dry goods merchants.)

America valued self-sufficiency and the autonomy of self-employment. The community looked down upon those who worked for wages. A young man might toil as a farmhand while waiting to acquire a holding of his own, or as a day laborer while learning a trade. A young woman might work as a domestic servant or teacher while waiting for a husband. Those who continued to labor for wages into later years bore the stigma of failure. The community defined success for a man as being a self-employed family head, with a farm, shop, store, or office of his own. For a woman, success meant being the wife of such a successful man, with a brood of children to help. The family formed the basic social unit. The person not part of a family was an outsider; he or she could rarely expect acceptance within the community.

Willy Bryan grew up in a large family with extensive community ties. While more prosperous than most, the Bryans probably fell close to the mean in many other ways. Born in Virginia of Scotch-Irish descent, Silas followed others of his family west, down the Ohio River. He scraped for an education, spending a few months at an academy in Missouri near the farm of his brother, William, for whom he later named his son. He then studied several years at McKendree College, a Methodist institution in Illinois, near the home of his sister, Nancy. He taught school while reading law, won election to a term as county superintendent of schools, secured admission to the bar, and, in 1852, married Mariah Jennings. Mariah gave birth to nine children, three of whom died before the age of five. Willy was born in 1860; he grew up with an older sister, two younger brothers (one of whom died at the age of seventeen years), and two younger sisters. Mollie Smith, orphaned niece of Silas and ten years older than the oldest Bryan child, lived with the family. Eventually Mariah's mother also came to live with the Bryans. Within Marion County lived many Jennings cousins, aunts, and uncles, and a number of Silas's relatives as well. Silas assisted with the legal careers of at least two of his nephews, taking one as a partner and bringing the other into his office to read law.

Next in importance to the family as a social institution stood the church. Salem counted eight churches during the years when Willy Bryan grew to manhood. Three were Methodist: one Northern, one Southern, and one for blacks. Both theology and regional sentiments separated the two Presbyterian congregations. Baptists, too, divided into two congregations, but along the lines of race. Salem also had a small Church of Christ. Catholics had formed a church during railroad construction in the 1850s, but only six Catholic families lived in Salem in 1881. Centralia, a town three times the size of Salem, held Marion County's only Catholic congregation large enough to support a priest. Few immigrants lived in Salem, only eight percent of the adults; old-stock Protestant churches—and values—dominated the town.

Divided by doctrine and sometimes by region, the Protestant churches of Salem—and most parts of the United States—nonetheless shared similar views on the nature of conversion, proper social behavior, and the role of the church. During the early nineteenth century, Methodists led the way in the development of an evangelical, perfectionist Protestantism that profoundly affected attitudes, if not formal doctrines, in most other denominations. The concept of free will infused Methodism with the belief that an individual could choose good or evil, rather than being predestined to one or the other. Through free will and the grace of God, the individual might cleanse sin from his or her life and be assured of salvation. By the time of the Civil War, the concepts of free will and perfectibility had found wide acceptance by the laity of most Protestant churches. Of the churches of Salem, only Old School Presbyterians and Catholics stood apart from these patterns.

Revivalism was the most widely practiced method for bringing people to the point at which they felt Christ enter their lives and change them forever. Baptists recognized this spiritual rebirth by adult baptism through total immersion. Cumberland Presbyterians considered a conversion experience necessary to become a communicant. For Methodists, this "second blessing" represented the inward assurance of success in cleansing sin from one's life. Revivalism typically took the form of a series of meetings filled with enthusiastic hymn-singing, lengthy prayers, and fervent preaching. Preachers held the center of attention, adjuring those already converted to maintain their faith and pleading with those not yet reborn to allow Christ to enter their lives.

Although the Protestants of Salem separated themselves into various denominations by disagreeing over the fine points of doctrine and practice, they acknowledged each other's legitimacy and cooperated in a variety of common endeavors. From 1843 to 1858, for example, the Baptists, Methodists, and Presbyterians of Salem jointly operated a Sunday school. From 1844 to 1858, when Baptists lacked a building, they met in the Cumberland Presbyterians' church. They moved into their own building in 1858, only to see it burn down during a revival held in it by the Cumberland Presbyterians, whereupon the Church of Christ offered the use of their building to the distraught Baptists. Such ecumenicalism extended to families as well. At haying time, Silas Bryan sent a load of hay to every clergyman in town, whatever his denomination. Because Silas was a Baptist and Mariah a Methodist, young Willy attended Sunday school twice each Sunday. He later claimed that it gave him a "double interest in Sunday-school work."

A broad agreement on definitions of acceptable social behavior further encouraged ecumenicalism among Protestants. Few Baptists or Cumberland Presbyterians would have disagreed with the list of unacceptable social conduct published by the Methodists in the late nineteenth century: "imprudent conduct, indulging sinful tempers or words, the buying, selling or using of intoxicating liquors as a beverage, signing petitions in favor of granting license for the sale of intoxicating liquors, becoming bondsmen for persons engaged in such traffic, renting property as a place in or on which to manufacture or sell intoxicating liquors, dancing, playing at games of chance, attending theaters, horse races, circuses, dancing parties, or patronizing dancing schools, or taking such other amusements as are obviously of misleading or questionable moral tendency." Such standards of conduct received strong endorsement in the Bryan household.

In the mid-nineteenth century, women often experienced conversion in larger proportions than men. Prevailing social views assigned women prominent roles in protecting moral standards and fostering proper conduct. Willy grew up surrounded by four older women, two of whom were devout Methodists. He never had a role model for behavior patterns his society assumed to be typically masculine—swearing, brawling, drinking, gambling. Silas was away from home for long periods of time on the judicial circuit; when at home, he reinforced the attitudes of the Bryan household's women on such behavior. Willy's childhood aversion to "improper conduct" developed into life-long commitments.

Willy's conversion came at the age of fourteen, when Salem's Cumberland Presbyterian Church held a series of revivals. The Cumberland Presbyterians rejected the doctrine that only a select few were predestined to salvation. He recalled in his *Memoirs* that "conversion did not mean a change in my habits of life or habits of thought." He did not find new theological truths nor did he "know of a virtue that came into my life as a result of joining the Church, because all the virtues had been taught me by my parents." Bryan remained a Presbyterian all his life, but he moved easily from the Cumberland denomination to a mainstream Presbyterian church when he left Salem. Retaining the ecumenicalism of his youth, he felt equally comfortable in other Protestant churches. Theological distinctions that separated denominations mattered less than personal commitment to

Christ and the belief that Christ had a similar commitment to each individual who accepted Him as Savior.

Silas Bryan opened his court with prayer, prayed three times each day, led his family in hymn-singing on Sunday afternoons, and brought his children catechisms as presents when he returned from holding court in another county. Young Willy deeply respected his father and emulated his religious habits. Silas Bryan's other great commitment was to the Democratic party of Thomas Jefferson and Andrew Jackson. This, too, young Willy absorbed and came to emulate. Silas Bryan won a variety of offices—county superintendent of schools and state senator before Willy was born, and circuit court judge and delegate to the 1869 constitutional convention during Willy's childhood. Just as the Bryan house often saw preachers or church leaders as guests, so too did it attract political figures. Silas Bryan held a Jeffersonian commitment to the people's right to, and capacity for, self-government. When Silas was young, Andrew Jackson had reformulated Jeffersonian ideals and added new dimensions to them. Professing a rough-hewn egalitarianism and fearing that active government usually meant granting economic privileges to a favored few, the followers of Jackson made minimal government their party's dominant theme during the years when Silas Bryan moved from Virginia to Illinois and sought elective office. "Too much government in republics," Silas once said, "is the rock upon which they founder." Willy disappointed his father when he rejected the Baptist church in favor of the Presbyterians, but no such apostasy marked his choice of political parties.

Observing and at times assisting in his father's campaigns, young Willy learned the mechanics of politics and the crucial role of political parties. Nominations for office, he learned, came from conventions that met frequently, before all elections. Convention delegates were chosen in caucuses, held at the lowest level of organization—rural townships or city wards. All Salem Democrats could attend the Democratic caucus and help select delegates to an upcoming county convention. County conventions—often held in the courthouse—made nominations for county offices and also selected delegates to nominating conventions for circuit court officers, state senators, members of Congress, or state officers. Party gatherings rarely convened with a majority committed to one candidate. Instead, conventions typically witnessed a series of roll calls and a great deal of informal bargaining, as leaders traded to build support for favorite candidates.

Once candidates secured nomination and the party wrote its platform, attention shifted to the voters. The party committee stood at the center of campaign activities, scheduling rallies, parades, and other activities to draw a crowd for their orators. Speakers held forth for an hour, two hours or more, praising their candidates and flaying the opposition; like revival preachers, they used the spoken word to strengthen the faith of their supporters and to convert unbelievers. The party raised campaign funds largely by asking candidates and patronage appointees for a percentage of the salary they received or hoped to receive. County committees usually subsidized at least one newspaper and expected it to serve as the party's voice throughout the campaign. On election day, as voters approached their polling places, they encountered eager party workers thrusting long strips of paper into their hands. A party symbol was emblazoned at the top of the strip, a rooster for the Democrats, an eagle for the Republicans; below that appeared the names of the party candidates. There were no secret ballots, no voting booths. To vote for the candidate of the Democratic party, a voter accepted a ticket from a Democratic party worker and deposited it in the ballot box inside the polling place. To vote Republican, he took a ticket from a GOP campaigner. Mobilization of supporters was the key to victory. Activists gauged their effectiveness by the ability to identify potential supporters and to get them to the polls.

The elaborate party organization did not go into hibernation after an election. Politicians agreed that "to the winner go the spoils," especially the right to fill appointive offices. Appointments to positions at every level—from courthouse janitors and prison guards to postmasters and pension agents—came from among the faithful party workers of the winning side. Men could rarely count on holding such jobs much longer than the term of the person who appointed them, but a host of applicants clamored for every available position. Legislative bodies—local, state, and federal—organized themselves along party lines, and party leaders played influential roles in guiding legislation. Judges—like Silas Bryan—also periodically stood for reelection as party candidates.

Most men felt strong party loyalties. Crossing party lines required the voter to cross out the name of the candidate on his party's ticket and then write in the name of the opposing party's candidate. "Scratching a ticket" occurred rarely. Most voters were partisans; the balloting system itself discouraged "scratching." Because women could not vote, they were seen as nonpolitical and hence as having no party loyalties. Having no party affiliation set a man apart as unusual and called into question his intelligence or masculinity; such a man might find himself characterized as effeminate, "a neuter gender," in the caustic words of one Kansas senator.

For most voters, party affiliation derived from attitudes related to social and economic characteristics. Ethnicity, religion, and party were closely related in much of mid-nineteenth century America. Outside the South, Republicans usually secured the support of three-quarters of the Methodists, Presbyterians, Congregationalists, and Northern Baptists. By contrast, Catholics usually voted Democratic in proportions of seven to one. Transplanted white southerners usually voted like their brethren in the South, giving strong support to the Democrats. Religion and sectional or national origin defined an outlook on the world which pushed its adherents, as a group, toward one of the political parties. Methodists, who believed in an obligation to perfect society, often saw government as one means of accomplishing that; one church publication defined "complete legal prohibition of the traffic in alcoholic drinks as the duty of civil government." Catholics and German Lutherans usually saw no sin in a glass of beer or a shot of whiskey; they considered alcohol a normal part of life, to be taken with meals or with friends. In contrast to the perfectionist leanings of the Methodists and Baptists, these groups believed that salvation came only through God's grace. Feeling no compulsion to perfect society, they regarded prohibition as a nativist assault on their lifestyle. Such groups usually affiliated with the Democrats, because Democrats showed a long history of opposing nativism, anti-Catholicism, and moral reform.

White Southerners after the Civil War usually voted the Democratic ticket. Willy Bryan came into the world a few months before Abraham Lincoln won election to the presidency. Lincoln's party, the Republicans, drew together Northerners who opposed the extension of slavery into the western territories, a few who favored outright abolition, some nativists fearful of increased immigration, and advocates of a stronger role for the federal government in the promotion of economic development. Southerners saw the election of Lincoln as a threat to their "peculiar institution"; one after another, state conventions voted to secede from the Union. Lincoln and his party defined the federal Union as indissoluble. The resolution of these differences came only after four years of Civil War. Few families escaped the loss or injury of a son, cousin, or neighbor.

Lincoln and the Republicans found little support in Salem. Early in 1860, the *Salem Advocate* condemned "the Black Republican sectional party," and that year Salemites voted sixty percent for Stephen Douglas, the Democratic candidate, and only twenty-seven percent for Lincoln. When war came, Silas Bryan did not volunteer as some prominent Salem political figures did. Leading citizens who volunteered often secured commissions as officers. Silas, the transplanted Virginian, wanted no part of the war. During the early months of 1861, as the *Advocate* carried news of the mustering of militia units to serve in the conflict, Silas won election as circuit judge. In 1863, after Lincoln issued the Emancipation Proclamation, Silas spoke out strongly against the continuation of the war and the politics of the Republicans. He admitted that the South "committed the first overt act of treason" and thereby bound "the whole North . . . to vindicate the Government," but he then argued that Lincoln and the Republicans had perverted the war from "preservation of the Constitution and Union" to "a free negro crusade." He voiced two demands: "First that [Lincoln] revoke his Emancipation Proclamation; and secondly, an *Armistice*—the suspension of hostilities." Many of the Bryans' neighbors shared Silas's dislike for freeing the slaves. In 1862, Illinois voted on a proposed change in the state constitution prohibiting voting by blacks; it carried Salem by 508 to 4. In 1864, when Lincoln sought reelection, Salemites again rejected their fellow Illinoisan.

Lincoln's defenders were no more numerous throughout surrounding counties. Salem stood near the edge of "Egypt" in southern Illinois, a triangular section with its apex pointed south, surrounded on two sides by slave states, Missouri and Kentucky. Census takers in 1870 found that more than a quarter of Salem's adults had been born in slave states. Salem lay geographically closer—and perhaps politically closer—to Arkansas and even Mississippi than to such abolitionist strongholds as Wisconsin or Ohio's Western Reserve. When Democrats such as Silas Bryan urged an end to the war and fulminated against emancipation, they drew heavy fire from the Republican administration. Democrats coupled criticism of the war and emancipation with charges that the conflict had resulted from machinations by New Englanders and that Western farmers suffered disproportionately from its effects. Western farmers lost Southern markets, lost their cheap water transportation route down the Mississippi River, and endured high railroad freight rates. Midway through the war, prominent Illinois Democrats, castigated as "Copperheads" by the Republicans, called for regulated railroad rates and an end to the practice of providing free railroad passes for elected officials.

The Civil War shaped political rhetoric and political behavior throughout the years when young Willy accompanied his father to rallies, listened to Fourth of July orations, and attended Memorial Day ceremonies. First proclaimed in 1868 as a time to honor the Union dead, Memorial Day soon became the Midwest's most important patriotic occasion and, coincidentally, an opportunity to suggest that all Democrats bore the stigma of disloyalty. Republicans canonized Lincoln and claimed a monopoly on patriotism for having saved the Union. "Every man that shot a Union soldier was a Democrat," declaimed one Republican campaigner in 1880. Union Army veterans were routinely importuned to "vote as you shot." Service in the Union Army, preferably as an officer, was *de rigueur* for Republican political candidates, and the GOP held out generous pensions to wounded Union veterans. In 1872, when Silas Bryan ran for Congress, he lost to a former Union Army general who was the federal pension agent in Salem. GOP orators derided the Democracy as the party of "the old slave-owner and slave-driver," but in the South secession became "the Lost Cause" and former Confederate officers took positions of prominence within the Democratic party.

From 1865 through the end of the century, Republicans claimed not just a monopoly on patriotism but also exclusive credit for economic growth. They pointed proudly to their party's support for land grants and to transcontinental railroads, for tariffs that fostered industrial development and high wages, for the Homestead Act, which gave free land to farmers, and for monetary and fiscal policies that maintained the nation's honor.

The common ground of Republican campaign rhetoric lay in the concept that government might appropriately serve limited purposes: to maintain the Union, to end slavery, to provide civil rights to former slaves, and to promote economic development by stimulating transportation, agricultural expansion, and industry. By contrast, the central tenet of the Democrats remained the Jacksonian belief that "government is best which governs least." They condemned the Republicans' tariff as class legislation, but had difficulty agreeing on an alternative. They accused Republicans of squandering the public domain by granting it to railroad corporations instead of reserving it for settlers. They opposed extending civil rights to former slaves, and described Republican policy as promoting "negro supremacy." This theme assumed special prominence in the South, where the Democrats typically called themselves the "white man's party" and advocated white supremacy. Beginning in 1876, Democratic national platforms carried commitments to "individual liberty," coupled with condemnations of prohibition and other such moral reforms.

The Democratic party of the 1870s and 1880s was a highly disparate coalition, composed of the South, which opposed any federal enforcement of the guarantees of the Fourteenth and Fifteenth Amendments; Catholics, German Lutherans, and other ethnic groups who opposed prohibition and moral reform; and Jacksonian ideologues, opposed to any economic privileges granted by government to any individual or class. One observer compared these diverse components to what "we see in the prairie-dog village, where owls, rattlesnakes, prairie-dogs, and lizards all live in the same hole." This awkward coalition sustained itself primarily because the members agreed that they did not want government to do hardly anything.

Politics formed a part of Willy Bryan's education from the beginning, but he later recalled that he became especially interested at the age of twelve, when his father sought election to the House of Representatives and when he accompanied his father to campaign rallies. He had started public school only two years before Silas ran for Congress. Before that, his mother had taught him at home, standing him on a small table to recite his lessons. Willy trudged three-quarters of a mile each day to school. In high school, he studied a classical curriculum. His participation in a debating club reinforced the emphasis on the spoken word, which he found in both church and in politics. Will probably learned as much from his parents as from his teachers and, after his second year in the Salem high school, Silas decided that his son needed a better education. He chose Whipple Academy, the preparatory branch of Illinois College in Jacksonville. Hiram Jones, a distant cousin, practiced medicine there and occasionally taught at the college. Will could live with Dr. Jones and his wife, saving on room and board expenses at a time when Bryan family finances felt the double pinch of Silas's retirement from the bench and national economic depression. Illinois College enjoyed a good reputation. Founded in 1830 by a group of Yale graduates, the college showed a strong New England influence.

Fifteen-year-old Will entered Whipple Academy as a "typical farmer lad with all the crudities that are characteristic of the species," according to the recollection of one of his instructors. Will spent two years in the Academy and four more at Illinois College, acquiring an education typical of many colleges of the day. The seven students in Bryan's class took nearly the same courses. Students received introductions to many subjects, but studied only languages in any depth; Bryan and his classmates had one year of German, three of Latin, four of Greek, and four of rhetoric (English composition and speaking). Bryan's education took place as much outside the classroom. Dr. Jones had wide-ranging intellectual interests and a large library, and Will learned from both. He helped edit the *College Rambler*, joined a literary society, mixed in campus politics, and belonged to the

Young Men's Christian Association. The budding orator also continued to hone his speaking abilities by participating in declamation contests. Until the fall of 1879, he paid attention to various young women at nearby academies; after that, he courted only one, Mary Elizabeth Baird, whose vitality and range of activities matched his own. A year later Will received the consent of Mr. Baird to marry his daughter. Their engagement was to prove lengthy, however; marriage had to wait until Will finished law school and could provide a home.

Silas hoped that Will could spend a year at Oxford University, in England, before beginning law school. He began saving toward that end, but he never lived to see his son graduate from Illinois College. In the spring of 1880, while visiting Will in Jacksonville, Silas suffered a stroke and died. Family finances took a serious downturn, although enough money remained for Will's law school tuition. In the spring of 1881, while Mary gave the valedictory at the Jacksonville Female Academy, Will delivered the valedictory at Illinois College. The student newspaper reported that "he intends to study law, making it the steppingstone to the arena of politics."

Will's law school years formed a stark contrast to the time he had spent in Jacksonville. He chose Union Law School in Chicago, probably the best in the area. Jacksonville had not proven much different from Salem, but Chicago seemed another world to the tall young man from Egypt. Will took an inexpensive room in a working-class part of the city, walked four miles to and from classes in order to save streetcar fare, and bought much of his food from pushcart peddlers and bargain lunch counters. On his walks through the city, Will passed extremes of wealth and poverty far greater than anything he had ever seen in Salem or Jacksonville.

While the family's savings paid Will's tuition, he earned room and board money by working as a clerk in the office of Lyman Trumbull, the most distinguished lawyer in Chicago, a former United States Senator, and one-time political confidant of Abraham Lincoln. Will also got to know Trumbull personally, not because he copied documents and swept out the office, but because Trumbull had been a political associate of Will's father and because Trumbull's son Henry was a fellow student at Union. From Lyman Trumbull, Bryan absorbed a hostility toward monopoly and concentrated wealth, an attitude for which his father's Jacksonianism had prepared the way and for which the great wealth and grinding poverty he witnessed daily made him all the more receptive.

Will learned as much from Lyman Trumbull and from his observation of the city as in his classes, thereby repeating patterns from Illinois College and school in Salem. Nonetheless, his disciplined study habits earned him good grades even as he managed to find time for the YMCA, church, and the presidency of the junior class. He also continued to improve his public speaking by taking part in school oratory contests. At the end of two years, when the class elected its valedictorian, Will missed the honor by a single vote.

With Will's graduation from law school, the only thing delaying marriage was the need to establish a law practice. Even before graduation, he had begun to examine prospective sites. Mariah wanted him to take his father's place in the office now run by two of Will's cousins but Will and Mary chose Jacksonville. Both of them had enjoyed their years there and both still had friends there. Dr. Jones helped by securing a place for Will in one of the town's leading firms. Will's practice developed slowly, however, consisting mostly of debt collections and insurance sales until one of the senior partners moved away and Will took some of his clients.

On October 1, 1884, Will and Mary recited their wedding vows. With financial help from Will's mother and Dr. Jones, they started building a house. Will spent a good deal of time during the first month of his married life in campaigning for Grover Cleveland, his party's candidate for president. Because the house was not yet complete, Mary lived with her parents in the nearby town of Perry. When they finally moved into their own home, Mary's parents moved in too; for as long as they lived, they remained with Will and Mary. Unlike most women of her day, Mary continued her studies after marriage, taking German classes and then law courses; she also participated in church functions and temperance societies. Will developed an adequate law practice at the same time that he took prominent roles in the YMCA, a lodge, the church, Sunday School, and temperance activities. A daughter, Ruth, was born a year after their marriage. Yet the choice of Jacksonville as home did not bring Will what he wanted most—the chance to seek elective office as a Democrat. He might take part in election speaking, but central Illinois voted as strongly Republican as Egypt had been Democratic.

A gnawing dissatisfaction with Jacksonville led Will to investigate other cities as possible sites for a practice. None seemed to hold more promise than Jacksonville. He sought a patronage position from the Cleveland administration, to no avail. Then, in July 1887, he traveled to Kansas to collect a debt for a client. He decided to stop on the return trip to visit a friend, Adolphus Talbot, who was practicing law in Lincoln, Nebraska. He spent two days with Dolph and came away convinced that the Bryans' future lay in Lincoln. The 1880s had witnessed rapid growth there. Lincoln's population doubled between 1885 and 1887, making it the fourth largest city west of the Missouri. As late as 1880, Lincoln had no paved streets, no water system, no sewers, no streetcars; by 1890 the city was to boast seventeen miles of paving, street lights along major thoroughfares, sewer connections to one house in five, a city water system, horse-drawn streetcars, and forty-six daily passenger trains that stopped in the city. A handsome new capitol building loomed over the southeast section of the city. Nebraska seemed to hold similar promise. Admitted as a state in 1867, its population had quadrupled between then and 1880 and was to double during the 1880s. In 1889, the state produced ten percent of the nation's corn crop.

Despite the bustle of rapid growth, in most ways Lincoln resembled Jacksonville more than it did Chicago. The same one- and two-story commercial buildings lined their main streets, although Lincoln could claim a six-story office building under construction, soon to house the offices of Talbot and Bryan. Lincoln took pride in its many Protestant churches, with Methodist and Presbyterian denominations the largest. The city also claimed thirteen temperance societies. Aside from some railroad shops and a few small manufacturing concerns, Lincoln contained little industry. It was, instead, a center for education and administration. The University of Nebraska campus lay only three blocks north of the business district. Just as Illinois College had raised the intellectual and cultural level of Jacksonville above that of other central Illinois towns, so the university promised to do the same for Lincoln.

In many ways, Lincoln and Nebraska seemed to hold greater potential than Jacksonville and Illinois. Will sensed that he had almost reached the "limit of possibilities" in Jacksonville, but believed the likelihood of continued rapid growth in Lincoln meant that a law practice could grow with the city. As the state capital, Lincoln held the prospect of a state supreme court practice, something not easily achieved in Jacksonville. One cloud darkened the horizon—Nebraska voted as solidly Republican as central Illinois, and the few pockets of Democrats lived mostly outside Lincoln. In his *Memoirs,* Bryan insisted that "every argument that impressed me was professional, no thought of politics ever entered my mind." Nonetheless, the Congressional district which included Lincoln had recently sent Nebraska's first Democratic Congressman to Washington. He had won through a split among Republicans, but the vote may have suggested to the young politician that Nebraska showed more political potential than central Illinois; certainly it was more attractive professionally. By September, Will was packing. He had determined to go ahead, get his law practice underway, and arrange for a house.

As Will and Dolph made their way through the bustling streets of Lincoln on October 1, 1887, it might have seemed that Bryan brought little to his new home on the plains. But within him he carried the values and attitudes formed in Salem, Jacksonville, and Chicago. He carried a deep reverence for family and church. He did not fight, drink, gamble, or swear. He believed that the Democratic party held the only hope for the nation, and that concentrated wealth posed the greatest danger to democracy and opportunity. And he still hoped to follow in his father's footsteps and pursue a career in elective office.

I I

The Populist Crusade

WILL BRYAN KEPT BUSY after his arrival in Lincoln. He initiated a new law practice in partnership with Dolph Talbot, arranged for a house to be built for his family, and established himself in the community. He slept in the law office in order to save money while carpenters toiled on the house, purchased through a loan from Mary's father. By the spring of 1888, the house stood ready and the entire family, including the Bairds, joined Will in Lincoln. Will and Mary moved easily into social and civic activities in their new home, quickly resuming church, lodge, temperance, and YMCA memberships. Mary was admitted to the bar in late 1888; in the summer of 1889, she gave birth to a second child, William Jennings Bryan, Jr. The Bryans established a new circle of friends, mostly young couples from among the town's professionals or from the University. Will built up his law practice in a shorter time than it had taken in Jacksonville; his speaking skills made him particularly successful in jury pleading. He also plunged into political speech-making for the Democratic party. He found campaign speaking not only temperamentally agreeable, but also a professional asset; he worked references to his law practice into his speeches, and he found clients as a result of stirring campaign addresses.

When Dolph met Will at the train station in 1887, he had introduced the newcomer to two Democrats before they left the depot. Will brought with him letters of introduction to prominent leaders of his party in Nebraska, including

J. Sterling Morton of Nebraska City. Morton invited Bryan to visit his home, Arbor Lodge, in early 1888; as they talked, Morton may have tutored the tall, young lawyer on the realities of Nebraska politics. Will could not have found a more knowledgeable mentor. Morton had arrived in Nebraska territory in 1855, won election to the territorial legislature within a few months, and later served as territorial secretary

Congressman-elect William Jennings Bryan, Mary Baird Bryan, and their children Ruth and William, November 1890. The youngest daughter, Grace, was born about three months later. (Photograph courtesy of the Nebraska State Historical Society.)

and acting governor. After statehood, Morton carried the Democratic standard repeatedly, albeit unsuccessfully. An ardent free-trader, Morton drew his following largely from outside Omaha.

Morton's chief rivals for party leadership lived in Omaha, Nebraska's largest city. Lincoln may have resembled an overgrown small town, but Omaha seemed like a miniature Chicago. Eastern terminus for the first transcontinental railroad and an important center for railroad traffic, Omaha's transportation advantages made it a regional center for finance and wholesale trade. The stockyards and packing plants of South Omaha heightened the resemblance to Chicago. Half the population of Omaha and South Omaha had immigrant parents or were immigrants themselves; Catholics outnumbered all the major Protestant denominations combined. Important Omaha Democrats included Gilbert M. Hitchcock, publisher of the *World-Herald,* the state's leading Democratic organ; John McShane, of Irish parentage, president of the Union Stock Yards Company, first Nebraska Democrat to win election to the House of Representatives, and unsuccessful candidate for governor in 1888; James E. Boyd, an Irishborn businessman and two-term mayor; and a host of other Irish businessmen and lawyers.

The typical Nebraska Republican leader, by contrast, hailed from a small town where he practiced law or ran a business. Two-thirds of them came to Nebraska after service in the Union Army. Most were from families that had been in the United States for several generations; nearly all were Protestants, with Methodists the most numerous. Many Republican voters closely resembled their leaders in ethnicity, but were joined by immigrants from Sweden and England. Republican campaign orators could always anticipate applause when they pointed to their party's passage of the Homestead Act. Nebraskans filed 116,169 claims under that act between 1863 and 1890; 45,293 claimants had received their final titles by the end of 1889, equivalent to two farms out of five in the state. Republican state officials did little beyond providing for local government, establishing state institutions, ladling out the patronage appointments associated with them, and occasionally encouraging development of some aspect of the state economy through subsidies or bounties. Despite recurring agitation throughout the 1880s for regulation of railroad freight rates, little was done.

While Nebraska Republicans resembled those of Illinois, most Democratic voters in Nebraska differed from the Democratic voters Bryan had known in Egypt. Few transplanted Southerners appeared on the rolls of the Nebraska Democracy; two-thirds of the state's Democrats were of foreign stock, either immigrants or the children of immigrants. Not all foreign stock groups voted Democratic; perhaps as many as one-third of Republican voters were also of foreign stock. But while Republicans got the bulk of votes from Swedes, Norwegians, and Protestants from Britain, Democrats ran most strongly among Irish, Czechs, and Germans. Throughout the 1880s, in a number of Middle Western states, these groups had become more and more solidly aligned with the Democrats as those states' Republicans moved in the direction of nativism and moral reform. In Iowa, in 1889, prohibition sentiment in Republican ranks produced the first Democratic governor since the Civil War. The next year, in Wisconsin, Democrats swept to victory by opposing a state law requiring Lutheran and Catholic parochial schools to use English in their classrooms.

In Nebraska, as in Iowa, Democratic candidates gained support among Catholics, German Lutherans, and others who opposed nativist or prohibitionist initiatives. In 1888, the Democrats of Nebraska won majorities in only a handful of counties, all of them strongly opposed to prohibition, all with large proportions of Irish, Germans, Czechs, or Poles. Democrats averaged less than a third of the vote in the counties most in favor of prohibition, all old-stock American or Swedish. J. Sterling Morton understood these important ethnic dimensions to Nebraska politics. In Irish communities, he concluded campaign speeches with a condemnation of "English tyranny"; before German audiences he pilloried Republicans for their part in establishing prohibition in Iowa and Kansas. He always mixed his appeals to ethnicity with an assault on Republican tariff policies.

Morton took an initial liking to Bryan, which the young lawyer reciprocated. Bryan, however, had been a tee-totaler all his life. A manuscript written in his hand on his Jacksonville letterhead testifies his views in the mid-1880s: "The man who drinks not only is unwise, but *sins*. He sins against himself, against those dependent upon him, against society and against his God. . . . Intemperance causes the great majority of our crime and poverty. It corrupts our politics . . ." Swayed by the realities of Nebraska politics and by the ideological arguments of "personal liberty" advocates like Morton, Bryan came to oppose moral reform in the late 1880s.

Bryan rose rapidly within a state Democratic party that had won only two significant elections in twenty years. By August 1888, he had to refuse pressures that he run for lieutenant governor or attorney general. The state committee asked him to speak throughout the state for the last several weeks of the 1888 campaign, and he did speak widely, tying support for the ticket to Morton's favorite topic, tariff reform. After one speaking engagement, he came home shortly before sunrise and excitedly awakened Mary. "I have had a strange experience," he told her. "Last night I found that I had power over the audience. I could move them as I chose. I have more than usual power as a speaker." He then prayed for Divine guidance that he might use his power wisely. Bryan played a major role in drafting the 1889 state platform, and soon party leaders approached him to run for the House of Representatives in 1890. Bryan agreed, thinking that he would at least make some acquaintances that would help his law practice. The 1890 election was to prove an unusual one. Temperance advocates finally succeeded in getting a Prohibition proposal placed on the ballot. And throughout the western half of the Middle West, farmers broke with both old parties and formed a new party: it was soon dubbed the Populist party.

Populism erupted like a volcano in 1890, forever changing the political landscape of Nebraska and surrounding states. Although casual observers may have assumed that it appeared from nowhere with dramatic suddenness, its origins lay a decade and more in the past. The years after the Civil War had brought problems to many farmers. They pushed westward, settling western Iowa, Minnesota, Kansas, Nebraska, and the Dakotas, drawn by the lure of free land through the Homestead Act or cheap land offered by railroads disposing of land grants. The number of farms in the South also increased, as large plantations gave way to smaller individual holdings. The number of farms in the nation grew from fewer than 2.5 million at the end of the Civil War to nearly 4.6 million in 1890. Many new farms specialized in one or two cash crops: cotton in the South, wheat or corn in the Midwest. Midwestern farmers who emphasized growing grain for cash sale came to feel themselves at the mercy of the grain buyer. Most small towns had only one or two grain buyers; they paid for grain on the basis of prices determined by the markets of Minneapolis and Chicago. Farmers complained that buyers paid them less than their grain was worth, but they knew no alternative buyer and had no way to store grain in hopes of better prices later. Farmers felt doubly at the mercy of the railroads, which hauled both their grain and the goods they had to buy. High freight rates, farmers believed, cut the returns on their crops and boosted the prices of what they bought. Railroad spokesmen defended their rates as reasonable and fair, but farmers found them exorbitant and blamed monopoly and greed.

The expansion of farming in Nebraska and elsewhere in the western Midwest came in major part on borrowed money. Farmers borrowed to buy land, supplies, seeds, tools, and livestock, even to live on, until the first crops came in. They secured loans easily in the late 1870s and early 1880s because Eastern investors considered farm mortgages a sound investment and eagerly sought to lend money on them. Farmers flocked to borrow. In 1890, census takers counted one mortgage for every two people in Kansas and North Dakota, one for every three in Nebraska, South Dakota, and Minnesota. Farmers plunged deeply into debt, often at steep interest rates, because they expected the land to produce enough to pay off the loan and to increase in value.

Moving west, buying unimproved land on credit, then working the land into a successful farm formed a pattern with deep roots in the American psyche. During the years after the Civil War, a flood of European immigrants made the dream their own. Borrowing money to create a farm of barren prairie *could* be a wise investment for the future. In the years after the Civil War, however, many farmers saw such sweet dreams go sour. Between 1866 and 1889, agricultural expansion and the emphasis on cash crops resulted in a 214 percent increase in corn production and a 175 percent expansion of wheat. The nation's population grew by only 69 percent. Despite a five-fold increase in the value of food products exported, the bulge in grain production when compared to population played a major role in forcing grain prices down. Corn sold for 66 cents a bushel in 1866, but brought only 28 cents in 1889. The price of wheat fell from $2.06 a bushel to 70 cents.

Falling grain prices magnified indebtedness. A farmer who borrowed $500 in 1881 for a term of five years at ten percent interest would have been required to pay the annual interest ($50) on the anniversary of the loan each year, and would owe the full principal at the end of five years. For the farmer, the most important measure of the debt was not the cash owed each year, but the crops it took to realize that cash. In 1881, 79 bushels of corn sold for $50. When a farmer first had to pay the annual interest, in 1882, falling corn prices required the sale of 104 bushels to raise $50. By 1885, it took 156 bushels to pay the annual interest. Falling prices required farmers to allocate more and more of their crops each year just to meet such fixed expenses as interest. As a result, farmers often had to renegotiate their loans at the end of five years, and annual interest payments continued or even increased. High railroad freight rates worked a similar hardship, for the cost of shipping grain did not fluctuate with grain prices; the higher the freight rates, the less farmers were paid.

In 1872, when Silas Bryan ran for Congress in Illinois, he secured not only the nomination of the Democrats but also that of a predecessor of the Greenback Party. Greenback candidates for president in 1876, 1880, and 1884 argued that the solution to farmers' economic problems lay in currency inflation, specifically in continuing to circulate "greenbacks," paper money first issued during the Civil War. The total circulating currency, including gold, silver, and paper, amounted to $30 per capita in 1865, but had fallen to $23 per capita by 1889. Greenbackers argued that this relative decline in the circulating currency contributed to falling prices and promoted an increase in the volume of currency. Greenbackers advocated more than currency inflation; their national platforms included a graduated income tax, the eight-hour day for wage-earners, abolition of child labor, regulation of freight rates, and woman suffrage. The Nebraska Greenbackers, a small but persistent group throughout the 1880s, often went beyond the national platform by calling for government ownership of the railroads in 1884 and for prohibition in 1886. A few farmers turned to third parties in the 1880s to seek relief from their economic problems, but most remained with the Republicans and Democrats, dividing along the axis of ethnicity rather than along economic lines.

The emergence and persistence of a series of small parties, all speaking to the problems of debtor farmers and also courting urban workers, paralleled the development of several ostensibly nonpartisan organizations among farmers. The most successful during the 1880s, the Farmers' Alliance movement, consisted of three separate organizations with the same name: the National or Northern Alliance, strongest in the Middle West; the Southern Alliance, which went through several name changes in the 1880s as it developed first in Texas and then spread throughout the South; and the Colored Farmers' National Alliance, an organizing adjunct of the all-white Southern Alliance. The Alliances combined social, economic, and educational functions. In Nebraska and other Middle Western states, local and state Alliances formed cooperative stores, grain elevators, and insurance plans. The educational activities of the Alliance included dissemination of information on new agricultural techniques and discussion of economic and political reforms. Local Alliances in Nebraska sometimes organized study groups and maintained circulating libraries. Alliance newspapers appeared at county and state levels. A Kansas woman claimed that because of Alliance activities, "people commenced to think who had never thought before, and people talked who had seldom spoken."

Although the Alliance defined itself as nonpartisan, some Nebraska Alliance members pursued political action from the beginning, using local third parties to win several county elections in 1881. In 1882, the state Alliance president ran for governor; another Alliance leader ran for governor in 1886. Their failure to win, the declining fortunes of the national Greenback party, and a brief plateau in the downward tumble of grain prices all combined during the mid-1880s to reduce interest in Alliance activities. Similar experiences affected the Northern Alliance in other states where it had made a promising beginning in the early 1880s. Ties between the leadership of the Northern Alliance and third party politics remained strong, however, and in 1888 the Union Labor Party (successor to the Greenback Party) nominated the president of the Northern Alliance as its presidential candidate.

In 1889, Nebraska cornfields produced large yields and corn prices dropped. Farmers soon realized that the bumper corn crop would bring them no more cash—perhaps less—than the lighter yields of previous years. In the midst of this frustration, the Republican state convention refused to re-nominate a supreme court judge who had antagonized rail-road corporations. Several county Alliances turned again to political action, naming their own tickets for county office that fall. Similar events took place in Kansas. All through the winter, Alliance members talked excitedly of an independent political course, and Alliance membership rolls burgeoned in anticipation.

In February 1890, when Democratic leaders approached Bryan to run for Congress, politically knowledgeable Ne-braskans anticipated a major political effort emanating from the Alliance. Kansas county Alliance presidents resolved in March "that we will no longer divide on party lines, and will cast our votes for the candidates of the people, by the people, and for the people." The next month, Nebraska county Alliance leaders met in Lincoln to discuss third party possibilities. State leaders held back, however, until local Alliance activists gathered 10,000 signatures on petitions calling for a new party. Kansas and South Dakota Alliance members formed parties in June and Nebraskans followed in July; by fall, Alliance-inspired parties had appeared in eight Middle Western states. Bryan understood the volatility of these political currents and courted Alliance members in his Congressional district. Nonetheless, when he accepted the Democratic nomination, he knew that the new Independent party had entrusted their Congressional nomination to the strongest possible candidate, Charles H. Van Wyck, erst-while leader of the anti-monopoly wing of the state Republican party and a former United States Senator.

Bryan campaigned hard and his supporters approached the Independents on his behalf. In September, Van Wyck withdrew and the Independents named a much weaker candidate. Observers now considered the election to be squarely between Bryan and the Republican incumbent, William J. Connell. The two debated the tariff in a number of joint appearances. The final joint debate drew a crowd so large that many had to be turned away. The real excitement of the 1890 election season, however, came not from the First Congressional District race but from the whirlwind Independent campaign and the furor created by the prohibition proposal.

Politics that summer and fall raged like the hot sun that glared down day after day, parching the corn crop in the field. Frustration and bitterness that had long smoldered now flared into defiance as thousands of farm families paraded their wagons down the dusty streets of a hundred towns, demonstrating their unity and their contempt for the bankers, lawyers, and merchants who watched from the wooden sidewalks. The parades culminated in rallies. There the farm families ate picnic lunches and put new words to familiar melodies:

> Worm or beetle, drouth or tempest,
> On a farmer's land may fall,
> But for first-class ruination
> Trust a mortgage 'gainst them all.

They also sang their condemnation of political parties that seemed oblivious to their distress:

> I was a party man one time
>   The party would not mind me,
> So now I'm working for myself,
>   The party's left behind me.

The rallies concluded with arm-waving speakers who attacked Wall Street, international bankers, monopolies, and the railroads. A Kansas woman described the 1890 campaign as "a religious revival, a crusade, a pentecost of politics"; and a Nebraska Democrat called it a composite of "the French Revolution and a western religious revival."

Three elements stand out in the third party's analysis of the political economy, although none may be claimed as a unique contribution. Nonetheless, the new party—known as Populists in Nebraska only after 1893 or 1894—popularized the creed and made impressive electoral gains. The first element traced its origins at least to Andrew Jackson, as Populist campaigners again and again proclaimed their opposition to concentrations of economic power. Jay Burrows, Nebraska Alliance leader, wrote that corporations had made "the toiling millions" into "the tools of a few plutocrats." Concentrations of economic power—railroads and grain markets were the most obvious to Nebraska farmers—posed dangers to economic opportunity for the individual, as well as to political liberty. Populist anti-monopoly sentiment might have met with understanding nods from seasoned Jacksonian Democrats, but the second element in Populist thought drew more from the Republican tradition of active government: Nebraska.Populists called for government ownership of the railroads and "all means of public communications." The state Alliance added government ownership of banks and coal mines. Government ownership of transportation, communication, and banking might restrain the aggressions of monopoly, but Populists argued—the third element in their analysis—that the people had to bring government itself more closely under their control. Populists proposed a range of reforms intended to increase voters' power over government decision-making, including the secret ballot, the direct election of United States Senators, and direct election of the President and Vice-President. Nebraska Populists also demanded currency inflation, whether by silver or paper, giving it first place in their early platforms.

Behind this analysis lay the concept of the producing class. The Farmers' Alliances shared with other late nineteenth century organizations, such as the Knights of Labor, a belief that they represented the "producers" of the nation. By this, they meant those people who by their labor produced value. If labor produced value, they reasoned, the producer might properly claim the full value created by that labor. "Wealth belongs to him who creates it," Populists proclaimed in their national platform of 1892. Bankers, merchants, lawyers, and grain buyers merely transferred wealth but did not produce value themselves. The Nebraska Alliance newspaper gave voice to the bitterness and frustration of a decade when it charged that "there are three great crops produced in Nebraska. One is a crop of corn, one a crop of freight rates, and one a crop of interest. One is produced by farmers who by sweat and toil farm the land. The other two are produced by men who sit in their offices and behind their bank counters and farm the farmers." As a result, "despite a generation of hard toil, the people are poor today, mortgage-ridden and distressed . . . They have produced but they possess not. They have amassed wealth for other people to enjoy while they themselves are almost without the necessities of life."

In 1890, while Bryan concentrated on his own Congressional campaign, he had to compete for the voters' attention not only with the political pyrotechnics of the Populists, but also with the equally dramatic fireworks of the campaign to ban the saloon. A few Republican spokesmen tried to make an issue of Bryan's own anomalous position on alcohol. His friends and neighbors knew him to advocate temperance and to abstain totally from alcohol; his party's platform, however, opposed any constitutional provisions affecting "the social habits of the people." The Democratic candidate for governor, James E. Boyd, devoted virtually his entire campaign to opposing prohibition. Throughout the 1890 campaign, Bryan accepted the position of his party: prohibition was undesirable and unnecessary because existing laws provided all appropriate regulation of the liquor trade.

Election day gave both Populists and Democrats cause to

celebrate. The Populists won majorities in both houses of the state legislature and took the Third District Congressional seat; a Populist with Democratic support won in the Second District. Boyd eked out a narrow victory for governor and Bryan won the First Congressional District. Republicans kept the loyalty of about 35 percent of the voters; Populists followed closely with 33 percent, and Democrats placed a close third with 30 percent. The Populists' strength among the voters came almost entirely from economically distressed farmers, regardless of ethnicity. Democratic candidates drew almost solely from the strongest opponents of prohibition, both in towns and in economically secure farming areas; economically distressed opponents of prohibition tended to vote Populist.

Bryan's victory immediately established him as one of the half-dozen most important Democrats in the state, although his official duties in Washington would not begin for more than a year after election day. State politics continued to flash and crackle like summer lightning on a Nebraska night. The state legislature met in Lincoln in January. The Populists who made up the majority soon revealed a serious lack of legislative experience; nonetheless, they passed an impressive array of legislation, including free textbooks for the public schools, legalization of mutual insurance funds, drought relief, and the secret ballot, printed and distributed by the government rather than by political parties. They also passed a bill establishing maximum railroad freight rates, but the governor vetoed it and the Populists could not override the veto.

The Bryan family had their attention diverted from the political spectacle at the capitol when, in mid-February, Mary gave birth to their third child, Grace. Perhaps because of this, the Congressman-elect played a minor role in party activities during the legislative session. By fall, however, the high stakes of state politics focused unusually close attention on the election for a state supreme court judge. All three major parties nominated candidates; after the conventions, however, the Democratic candidate withdrew. Bryan joined Hitchcock and Boyd in urging the state committee to leave the party ticket vacant as a way of freeing Democrats to vote for the Populist candidate. After acrimonious debate, the committee did so. This first state-wide foray into Democratic support for the Populists failed to accomplish its purpose; Democratic voters split their votes largely along the lines of economic status and the Republican candidate won by a narrow margin.

While the 1891 election enlivened the weeks before Bryan left for Washington to take up his Congressional duties, he also ventured beyond Nebraska politics. He spoke in Iowa for reelection of the Democratic governor, and he traveled to Ohio to speak against the election of William McKinley, erstwhile leader of Congressional high-tariff advocates and now the GOP candidate for governor. Above all, Bryan spent the year between his election and his seating in a study of two issues: the tariff and the currency. He already felt at home with the general principles of the tariff; he now needed to master the intricacies of legislation. He had not yet developed more than a cursory position on currency issues. When elected in 1890, he had run on a platform favoring "free coinage of silver on equal terms with gold," but had said little else on the subject. Throughout 1891, he moved slowly in the direction of those favoring currency inflation through silver coinage. In his mind, however, silver had not assumed the status of a leading issue; tariff reform still held first rank for him. He pushed for a silver plank in the 1891 state Democratic platform and got part of what he wanted. As Bryan moved in the direction of silver, however, he moved away from the guidance of J. Sterling Morton and into opposition to most of the older generation of Nebraska Democrats.

The new Democratic Congressman from Nebraska impressed some Washingtonians as a "hayseed," but soon they changed their views. His strong support of William Springer for Speaker brought him a position on the influential Ways and Means Committee, one of the most important committees in the House, and the perfect platform for an assault on the tariff. Mary and Will formed a strong team on Capitol Hill. They had modest rooms near the Capitol but took little part in the city's social life. Mary experienced difficulty with appropriate fashion for Washington occasions, but in the view of the *Washington Post,* "her judgment was excellent." She followed public issues carefully. She and Will worked on speeches together; when Will rose to speak on the floor of the House, Mary sat in the visitors' gallery, coaching him by nodding her head or signalling disapproval.

Bryan got his first chance for a major floor speech in mid-March 1892, in defense of a Democratic proposal to reduce the tariff on wool. He seized the opportunity and moved rapidly from the specifics of the bill to general principles. With Mary coaching from the gallery, he held forth for three hours, marshaling his physical strength, wielding the debating skills honed through long years of speaking, and filling the chamber with the carefully rehearsed cadence of his magnificent voice. He presented no new concepts but instead took long-standing arguments and presented them in such eloquent fashion that New York newspapers splashed his name and speech across front pages. One paper proclaimed that the speech would "compare favorably with anything that has ever been delivered in the halls of Congress." Bryan's oratorical talents, long practiced in the courtroom and on the hustings, now lifted him from the ranks of anonymous Congressional freshmen and put him in a leadership position in the tariff reform fight.

Bryan accomplished more during his first term than a magnificent speech on the tariff. He looked after the interests of his constituents and introduced several unsuccessful bills, including proposals for the direct election of United States Senators and elimination of tariff protection from items made by trusts or monopolies. One of his bills, to require greater publicity for federal court orders foreclosing land mortgages, became law. He made a point of meeting every member of the House of Representatives, including leaders of the emerging Populist Party. From his new vantage point in Washington, he could watch with interest as the Alliances and state parties of 1890 moved to become a national political party.

In May 1891, a meeting in Cincinnati announced the creation of a new national party and set a timetable for nominating a presidential candidate in 1892. When the nominating convention met in Omaha in July 1892, the reading of the platform provoked an outburst so great that one reporter compared it to French revolutionaries storming the Bastille. "The fruits of the toil of millions are boldly stolen to build up colossal fortunes for a few," the Omaha platform declared. It then demanded that "the powers of the government—in other words, of the people—should be expanded (as in the case of the postal service) as rapidly and as far as the good sense of intelligent people and the teaching of experience shall justify, to the end that oppression, injustice, and poverty shall eventually cease in the land." Among its proposals, the platform gave first place to the creation of a "safe, sound and flexible" currency through silver coinage. Other planks included a graduated income tax, government ownership of railroads and telegraph and telephone systems, the secret ballot, the eight-hour work day, and the abolition of private "armies" used in breaking strikes. Their candidate for president, James B. Weaver, had reached the rank of general in the Union Army during the Civil War, and had run for president as the candidate of the Greenback Party in 1880. For Vice-President, the Populists chose a former Confederate officer, symbolically healing the division that had separated North and South since 1865 and uniting the sections on the basis of an economic program that spoke to the economically distressed.

While Bryan watched these proceedings from a distance,

he had a more immediate stake in the decisions of his own party. In April 1892, Nebraska Democrats met to select delegates to the presidential nominating convention. Supporters of Grover Cleveland held tight control, and they opposed Bryan's views on silver. When Bryan submitted a silver amendment to the platform, he lost on a close and disputed vote. He nonetheless won renomination easily in July and ran on a personal platform that emphasized silver coinage. Morton took his fourth nomination for governor, more to solidify his claim to party leadership than in the hope of winning. The platform said not a word about the silver issue.

Bryan once again went to the voters with a conflict between his personal views and his party's platform. In 1890, he had advocated the party position on prohibition despite his own views on alcohol. In 1892, however, he followed his own course and campaigned for reelection as an advocate of silver; he continued to stress tariff and income tax issues. The 1891 legislature had redistricted the state in accordance with the 1890 census; the new First District showed a larger normal Republican majority than before. Bryan could win only by attracting most of the Populist voters. His opponents made the task somewhat easier. His Republican opponent could not match Bryan's oratorical prowess, and a series of debates between them merely allowed Bryan to demonstrate his eloquence. The Populist candidate lost ground when his supporters discovered that he had accepted campaign donations from the Republicans. Voters drew the conclusion that the GOP wanted the Populist to draw votes from Bryan. Eastern Republicans contributed $20,000 to defeat Bryan. Described by one newspaper in 1890 as "able, brilliant, young, magnetic, hopeful, candid, honest, and poor," Bryan used his own voice as his best campaign resource, though he also sent a supporter to raise $4,000 from silver mining interests in Colorado and Utah. He made no secret of his preference for Weaver in the presidential contest, but he admitted that, as a "born Democrat," he would vote a straight Democratic ticket. He did *not* ask anyone else to vote for Cleveland. The state party leadership eventually came to the same position. In late October, only ten days before the election, the state committee urged all Nebraska Democrats to vote for Weaver as the only possible way of denying Nebraska's electoral votes to the Republicans.

The results showed the failure of Morton's strategy of tying the state Democratic party tightly to the conservatism of Cleveland. Many Democratic voters bolted to the Populists, though Bryan garnered enough Populist votes to eke out a narrow victory. He was the only Democrat in the state to win a significant office. Democrats in the state legislature found themselves a tiny minority, but a minority that held the balance of power in both houses.

The state legislature was to elect a member of the United States Senate; the two houses met in joint session for that purpose. Republicans counted 62 members, Populists 53, and Democrats only 18. Election of a senator required a majority. In previous years, leading Democrats had made proposals for cooperation between their party and the Populists, but until the 1893 legislative session, Populists gave no indication of welcoming Democratic support. During the 1893 legislative session, the two parties moved toward coalition. Although the Congressional session required Bryan's presence in Washington, he maintained close contact with events in Lincoln.

Balloting for senator began early in the session, but five weeks elapsed before a candidate received a majority. Bryan had solid support among some Democratic legislators, and he hoped he was to be an acceptable second choice for the Populists. He also considered that he might swing enough votes to a Populist candidate to claim the role of kingmaker. Three weeks into the session, the Populist legislative caucus supported John H. Powers; Bryan's allies found Powers unacceptable because of his reputation as a rigid moralist who understood little about politics. In early February, however, the Populists changed to William V. Allen. A lawyer and a district judge, he had been active in Van Wyck's wing of the state Republican party before 1890 and had followed Van Wyck into the Populist fold. Allen immediately met with the Bryan Democrats and agreed to work closely with Bryan. Bryan's supporters promptly gave their votes to Allen, but five conservative Democrats held the balance. Bryan persuaded several prominent Democratic senators to send telegrams to the five, urging support for Allen. Eventually all five did so. Allen assured Bryan that he realized his election came from Bryan's efforts and that he would repay the debt in the future.

After Congress recessed in early 1893, Bryan filled speaking engagements in the West and South, usually concentrating on the silver issue. The state convention in the fall voted by three to one against even giving Bryan a seat on the Resolutions Committee. Part of the opposition came from the large Omaha contingent and part from J. Sterling Morton, whom President Cleveland had recently appointed Secretary of Agriculture. Because Morton was to control federal patronage for Nebraska, delegates hoping for a federal patronage slot followed his directives to punish the brash young Congressman, whose recent speaking tour had opposed the president's currency policies. The platform and candidates were wholly supportive of Cleveland, and Nebraska Democratic voters responded by continuing their exodus from the party. Bryan understood clearly that only a change in the course of the state party would salvage his own political career.

Before he could give full attention to state politics, however, Bryan had to return to Washington for the first session of the Fifty-third congress. He continued on the Ways and Means Committee, and once more played a key role in the floor debate on a crucial measure. Many Democrats advocated an income tax as a means of replacing revenue lost by lowering the tariff; they proposed a tax rate of two percent on all income over $4,000 per year. The choice of Bryan to defend the measure points to the high regard in which his colleagues held his oratorical abilities. Bryan proved equal to the occasion. He announced his personal preference for a graduated tax, but supported the proposal as better than no income tax at all, for "there is no more just tax upon the statute books than the income tax, nor can any tax be proposed which is more equitable." Near his conclusion, he derided his opponents and defended the tax supporters: "They call that man a statesman whose ear is tuned to catch the slightest pulsations of a pocket-book, and denounce as a demagogue anyone who dares to listen to the heart-beat of humanity."

As Bryan laid his plans to capture the Nebraska Democratic Party in 1894, he found assistance from a most unexpected quarter. In late August, the Republican state convention gave its nomination for governor to Thomas J. Majors. A Union Army veteran, Majors took an active role in the Grand Army of the Republic (the leading veterans' group); he also maintained close connections with the Burlington railroad and equally close ties to the American Protective Association (APA). The APA exerted a good deal of influence in the 1894 Republican convention. Majors may or may not have actually paid dues to the organization, but the APA praised him and he refused to criticize them.

Begun in 1887 in eastern Iowa, the APA was founded on the proposition that Catholics posed a danger to the nation and that Protestants had to unite behind the APA banner to counter this threat. Members took solemn oaths never to vote for a Catholic, never to patronize a business run by Catholics, never to hire a Catholic employee, and to do everything possible to dislodge Catholics from positions of public trust. In 1891, the APA took control of the Republican organization in Omaha and pushed its slate to victory. Within a year, the secret order claimed most Omaha city officials as members. Nebraska Democrats denounced the secret order as "un-American," "treasonable," and "cowardly" in 1891, and repeated variations on those themes in 1892 and 1893. In 1893, the Populists joined in the attack on the secret order with a platform plank that opposed "religious tests for office" and condemned "all secret or open religious organizations based on religious prejudices." They repeated the condemnation in 1894 and nominated Silas Holcomb, a lawyer and former Democrat, for governor.

In late June 1894, an Omaha meeting produced the Nebraska Democratic Free Coinage League, the organizational structure through which Bryan's forces hoped to control the convention. Bryan and his supporters made clear their intention to give Holcomb the Democratic nomination if they could control the state convention. Omaha Democratic leaders found themselves on the horns of a most uncomfortable dilemma. As Irish-Catholics, they could not accept having a known anti-Catholic as governor; as successful businessmen, they felt no particular desire to see a Populist in the Statehouse. They dodged the dilemma by stepping aside and letting Bryan's forces fight it out with Cleveland's patronage appointees. Bryan's Omaha allies selected a carefully balanced ticket and swept the city's delegation. The state convention found Bryan's forces in the majority. Bryan himself proposed Holcomb, and the convention gave him their nomination on the first ballot. Bryan received unanimous endorsement for the United States Senate and the convention enthusiastically shouted through a commitment to free silver. The remainder of the platform demanded an income tax, government ownership of the telegraph system, and government ownership of all transcontinental railroad lines then in bankruptcy. Bryan had brought fusion to Nebraska.

The campaign rhetoric of 1894 waxed extremely bitter. Edward Rosewater, a prominent Republican, bolted his party and used his newspaper, the *Omaha Bee* to label Majors a tool of the railroad and charge him with a long list of corrupt actions. Catholic voters—who usually voted Democratic—proved crucial to Holcomb's narrow victory. Bryan chose not to seek a third term in Congress—he may have seen his 140-vote margin in 1892 as an ominous forecast— but instead he invoked an obscure provision of the election code to have his name listed on the ballot as a candidate for the United States Senate. The vote for this position carried no legal effect on the legislature, which elected Senators; the sole purpose of the vote was to indicate popular support. Republicans and Populists refused to name candidates. Bryan's only opponent was the nominee of the Prohibition party. He got three-fourths of the votes cast for senator, but nearly half the voters ignored the popularity contest. Republicans swept all offices except governor, and—deathblow to Bryan's senatorial hopes—took three-to-one majorities in both houses of the legislature.

Bryan now stood at a crossroads. During the seven years since he met Dolph Talbot at the Lincoln train depot, he had parlayed his splendid speaking voice and enthusiasm for the Democratic party into leadership within a state organization demoralized by its perpetual inability to win office. Offered the chance to carry the party banner in what most considered a hopeless contest for Congress, he seized the opportunity and won, aided by the emergence of Populism. In Congress, he mustered his oratorical talents to achieve national attention, undertook speaking engagements around the country, and became a leader in the silver cause. His splendid baritone voice, engaging smile, and magnetic personality brought him a set of loyal supporters, especially among younger Democrats. Realizing that neither Populists nor Democrats could win major office on their own in Nebraska, he threw Democratic support to attractive Populist candidates and guaranteed their election as senator and governor. He challenged the thirty-year masters of the state Democratic party and wrested it from their control. He had a host of admirers within the Democratic and Populist parties; important officeholders owed him a debt for their

election. Although his two Congressional terms laid the
foundation for a national following, his failure to take the
Senate seat raised questions for the future.

The day the election results became known, Mary asked
Will to grant her one request. He replied, "Mary, you know
that anything in life that I can do for you, I will gladly do,
unless you ask me the impossible." She asked him to settle
down to his law practice and to writing, and to stop traveling
about the nation on political errands. "You can make a comfortable living," she coaxed, and added, "It will be more
pleasant for you, me, and the whole family." Bryan acknowledged the truth of her arguments, but then told her
that she asked the impossible. "It would seem to me as if I
were born for this life," he explained, "and I must continue
to fight the battles of the people, for what I think is right
and just, if I have to do so single-handed and alone. I care
naught whether I am ever elected to an office or not."
Within a few days, he received a letter from Jim Dahlman,
an officer of the Free Coinage League, who announced that
"I have begun to talk you for President . . . No gift in the
hands of the people is too high for you."

Presidential candidate William Jennings Bryan on the campaign trail, 1896. (Photograph courtesy of the Nebraska State Historical Society.)

I I I

The First Battle: Crusade for Free Silver

IF WILLIAM JENNINGS BRYAN had paused when he received Jim Dahlman's letter, and considered his course of action over the next eighteen months, he might have started with the "lame duck" session of the Fifty-third Congress, which was sure to keep him in Washington until spring. While there, he would continue to write editorials for the *Omaha World-Herald*, a practice he had begun in September 1894. Gilbert M. Hitchcock, the publisher, had offered to list Bryan as editor-in-chief and to publish his political commentary; in return, Bryan was to invest $25,000 in the paper. Bryan came up with $2,000. His father-in-law and some Nebraska political supporters raised the total to $9,000. Hitchcock apparently decided to forego the remainder. Bryan had originally intended to use his editorial opportunity to promote his election to the Senate; once the legislative election results dashed those hopes, he continued to present short political articles—and draw a small salary—until mid-1896. He thought of resuming his law practice when the Congressional session came to a close, but had also grown fond of delivering speeches throughout the nation. In addition to these prospects, he must have anticipated that his control of the Nebraska Democratic Party would come under challenge, and that he would have to work at maintaining the coalition he had forged in 1894. Finally, he could not have

49

avoided the realization that his thirty-fifth birthday, in March 1895, would make him constitutionally eligible for the presidency.

The lame duck session of the Fifty-third Congress produced no major legislation, so Bryan used his time in Washington to promote what had become for him *the* political issue. Toward the end of the session, he prepared an address directed to the Democrats of the United States, calling upon silver supporters to "take charge of the party organization and make the Democratic party an effective instrument in the accomplishment of needed reforms." Thirty-one congressmen signed. Richard Bland, long-time leader of Congressional silver advocates, put his name at the head of the left column; at the top of the right column was boldly scrawled "W. J. Bryan." In the address, Bryan proclaimed that "the money question will be the paramount issue in 1896."

An understanding of the "money question" must begin with the act establishing the United States Mint in 1792, which stated that the Mint should accept gold and silver bullion and make it into coins of specific weights. The amount of silver in a silver dollar would weigh exactly fifteen times more than the amount of gold in a gold dollar. The Mint did not *purchase* gold and silver, but instead coined bullion presented to it. "Free and unlimited coinage of gold and silver," therefore, meant that the Mint would take unlimited quantities of bullion and coin it without charge. Unfortunately, the 15–1 ratio set too low a value for gold in comparison with that set by European nations. Holders of silver bullion outside the United States found it advantageous to exchange it for American gold and return the gold to their own country. Gold rapidly left the nation and the country soon found itself on a de facto silver standard. In 1834, Congress changed the ratio to 16–1, which undervalued silver. By 1853, there were no silver coins in circulation because silver had more value as a commodity than as money. The United States had moved onto a de facto gold standard.

In 1873, during a recodification of the coinage laws, the silver dollar quietly disappeared from the list of authorized coins. In some part, dropping the silver dollar simply recognized reality. But those who drafted the new law knew things that most members of Congress did not know. Massive silver discoveries in the West would soon drive the commercial price of silver below the 16–1 ratio; when that happened, silver would again flow to the Mint and the nation would rapidly return to a bimetallic standard. Dropping the silver dollar from the list of authorized coins would keep the nation on a de facto gold standard; they believed this would improve the nation's commercial and financial position vis-à-vis other nations. This action, largely ignored at the time, was soon to be labeled the "Crime of '73" and to occupy an important place in the demonology of the silver movement.

Within a few years, the demonetization of silver became a political issue. In 1878, Congress passed the Bland-Allison Act over the veto of President Rutherford B. Hayes; the measure provoked a sectional split within Congress, with most votes in favor coming from the West and South. This act, which earned for Richard Bland his sobriquet "Silver Dick," represented a compromise between the advocates of unlimited silver coinage and those who wanted to restrict silver money. The act required the government to buy a limited amount of silver bullion each month and to coin it into silver dollars. The act satisfied neither those who wanted a bimetallic standard nor those who favored gold. As a result, the Republican Congress in 1890 replaced it with the Sherman Silver Purchase Act. This proposal, an attempt to satisfy western Republican silverites without enacting unlimited coinage, required the government to buy a fixed dollar value of silver each month and pay for it with legal tender notes, redeemable in either gold or silver. The Mint would coin no more silver dollars. The Sherman Act produced no greater consensus than the act it replaced; in 1893, President Cleveland asked Congress to repeal it. The repeal carried, with Democrats providing most of the opposition.

By the late 1880s, much of the inflationist sentiment that fueled the Greenback movement came to embrace silver as an inflationary device through which to secure broader support than paper money could attract. (One wag claimed the silver advocates wanted "honest money and lots of it.") Those who favored inflation accepted the quantity theory of money and prices. Money, they argued, followed the rules of supply and demand: the less of it in circulation, the greater its value; the scarcer money became, the more it would buy and the lower prices would drop. Leading economists disagreed on the functioning of the monetary system and its relation to price levels. Some accepted the quantity theory, others maintained that falling prices resulted primarily from increased productivity. Gold standard supporters complained that silver coinage would raise prices; silverites responded that without silver coinage, prices would continue to fall and would work a greater hardship on debtors.

Bryan moved slowly to his position that silver was the paramount issue. He paid it little attention in 1890, but he studied the currency issue in depth following his election. In a speech early the next year, he tied the currency issue to both debt and Western regionalism. "We simply say to the East," he told a Kansas City crowd, "take your hands out of our pockets and keep them out." By the fall of 1891, he had fully accepted the arguments of Bland and other silverites that 16–1 was the appropriate ratio, and he announced that he was willing to speak by invitation on "low tariff, anti-prohibition, and, if you like, free coinage." Silver slowly climbed up his list of priorities through 1892, although, as late as September, the *World-Herald* quoted him as saying: "I don't know anything about free silver. The people of Nebraska are for free silver and I am for free silver. I will look up the arguments later." Bryan had long since looked up the arguments and by 1893 he fixed on silver as the issue that most distinguished his faction from the Cleveland Democrats who controlled the Nebraska Democratic party. That fall in St. Louis, he accused the gold standard advocates of wanting to make "a man pay a debt with a dollar larger than the one he borrowed. . . . They loaned money, and now they want more than they loaned." The platform Bryan wrote for the Nebraska Democratic party in 1894 argued that the government should "make the dollar so stable in its purchasing power that it will defraud neither debtor nor creditor."

Bryan's growing attraction to silver coincided with a nationwide movement in the same direction. Between 1889 and 1893, the silver cause attracted such diverse groups as silver mining interests, Populists and others concerned with the problems of debtor farmers, prominent Democrats from the South and West, a few officers of labor organizations, some businessmen, and leading Republicans from silver-mining states. Midway through 1894, William H. Harvey published *Coin's Financial School,* a fictional account of a series of lectures by a young silver defender whose logic confounded the most prominent financial and commercial figures of the day. As the book quickly became a best seller across the nation, it gave a further boost to the booming silver cause. Bryan publicly recommended the book to President Cleveland in response to the president's demands for "sound money." In early 1896, the three leading national organizations favoring silver coinage joined to call for a Silver party convention following the Republican and Democratic nominating conventions.

When the Fifty-third Congress adjourned in the spring of 1895, Bryan was riding the crest of the silver wave. A flurry of requests that he speak around the country overwhelmed earlier thoughts of resuming his law practice. From March 1895 to July 1896, he traveled throughout the South and West, carrying the message of silver and coupling it to other reforms. He sought out the political leaders of all parties and factions who seemed to lean toward silver, and followed up his visits with letters and copies of his speeches.

On New Year's Day 1896, Bryan wrote to prominent Populists urging a union of all silver advocates in the upcoming presidential campaign. He also suggested that the Populists hold their national nominating convention after the Republicans and Democrats had met. If both major parties rejected silver, the Populists could recruit a host of silver Democrats and a smaller number of silver Republicans. General James B. Weaver, the 1892 Populist presidential candidate, shared Bryan's concern that the silver forces act in harmony; the Populist national committee accepted their logic. The Silver party and the Populists adopted the same schedule for their nominating conventions. In prompting the Populists to hold a late convention, Bryan probably cherished another scenario than the one he had presented to the Populists. He hoped that the Democrats would nominate a silver advocate; if that happened, it would be essential that there be no competing Populist silver ticket in the field. Nearly two months earlier, Bryan had confided to a close political ally that he considered his own nomination possible if silver Democrats controlled their party's convention.

By late January, Bryan turned increasingly to the elements essential to realization of his goal. First, silver delegates must comprise the majority of the Democratic convention. Second, they must remain uncommitted to any of the leading candidates. Bryan tirelessly pushed both goals in his speaking and writing. The Nebraska convention of Bryan's wing of the party adopted a platform calling for silver, the income tax, direct election of senators, and the initiative and referendum; the long closing paragraph attacked the APA. After the convention adopted its platform and chose delegates, Bryan's friend, Jim Dahlman, moved to instruct the delegation for Bryan. Bryan demurred and asked that the motion be withdrawn. This self-denying action then became a lesson for other favorite sons. By advocating that states send delegates committed to silver but not committed to candidates, Bryan knew that he was making it difficult, perhaps impossible, for any candidate to come to the convention with the two-thirds majority necessary to take the nomination. At the same time, his mail brought offers of support from across the South and West. When all the delegates had been chosen, silver claimed the majority and most delegates had found a complete set of Bryan's speeches in their mailboxes.

While Bryan bent all his efforts toward keeping the Democratic convention open, William McKinley was tightly locking up the Republican gathering. Bryan attended the GOP convention, in St. Louis, as a reporter for the *World-Herald*. McKinley had put together a strong campaign for the nomination, based in the Middle West, but with important strength nearly everywhere. He portrayed his campaign as a struggle by the people against party bosses. Author of the highly protectionist tariff of 1890, McKinley delighted in presenting himself as his party's leading tariff expert and in blaming the Democratic tariff for the depressed economic conditions of the Cleveland years. Throughout his career, the tariff had been McKinley's forte and he hoped for a campaign in 1896 with the tariff as the central issue. He straddled the money question until a few days before the convention when he and his advisers decided to write into the platform a commitment to "the existing gold standard."

The Republican convention bore marks of scrupulous organizing by McKinley forces, directed by Marcus A. Hanna, a retired manufacturer and delegate from Ohio. Virtually the only change in the carefully scripted proceedings came when Henry Cabot Lodge of Massachusetts secured a platform addition proposing to establish the bimetallic standard through international agreement. The gesture failed to placate silver Republicans. When the convention adopted the gold plank, Senator Henry Teller of Colorado led a group of delegates out of the convention hall and out of their party. The departure of their western brethren caused the remaining delegates to miss not a single step in their march to nominate McKinley on the first ballot. Though most political observers had anticipated the bolt of the silverites, it still delighted Bryan, for it gave every indication of fulfilling his hope for unification of all the silver forces.

One of McKinley's key organizers, a young Chicago lawyer named Charles G. Dawes, had recently moved to the Windy City from Lincoln, where he had been well acquainted with Bryan. Dawes told Hanna that both presidential candidates would have the same first name if Bryan somehow managed to address the Democratic convention. Hanna reassured him that McKinley expected the Democrats to nominate Bland. For a time it appeared that Dawes's condition—that Bryan address the convention—might not come about. The pro-Cleveland National Committee gave Nebraska's seats to a contesting delegation committed to the gold standard. Bryan and his delegation could not be seated until the convention officially opened and voted on the Credentials Committee report. As a result, Bryan lost several opportunities to speak during the early phases of the convention. As soon as he and his delegation were seated, however, he set off for the room where the platform was being drafted. The committee chairman, Senator James K. Jones of Arkansas, asked the Nebraskan to defend the platform in a debate before the convention. Charles Dawes's reputation for political prediction was soon to be tested.

The convention took up the platform before it turned to nominating candidates. The committee designated two members to speak in support of the platform, Senator Benjamin Tillman of South Carolina and Bryan. Tillman wanted to close debate, but Bryan persuaded him to lead off instead. Bryan later recorded: "I was more effective in a brief speech in conclusion than in a long speech that simply laid down propositions for another to answer." Bryan sat with his delegation on the floor of the convention, sucking a lemon to clear his throat, while Senator Jones read the platform. Tillman harangued the convention for nearly an hour, but the delegates quickly tired of his vituperations. Three opposition speakers came next. Senator David B. Hill of New York coldly defended Cleveland's gold policies and condemned the platform as "unnecessary, ridiculous, and foolish." Senator William F. Vilas of Wisconsin followed, but his speech failed to ignite much enthusiasm. William E. Russell, former governor of Massachusetts, was in poor health and had difficulty making himself heard. When Russell finished, Bryan sprang from his seat and bounded to the platform. He raised his right arm and bade the crowd be quiet. An electric current of anticipation rushed through the hall as the silver delegates eagerly waited for Bryan to put their emotions into words. He did not fail them.

"I would be presumptuous indeed," Bryan began, "to present myself against the distinguished gentlemen to whom you have listened if this were a mere measuring of abilities." He had used such modest disclaimers before, as a means of emphasizing issues rather than personalities. "This is not a contest between persons. The humblest citizen in all the land, when clad in the armor of righteous cause, is stronger than all the hosts of error. I come to speak to you in defense of a cause as holy as the cause of liberty—the cause of humanity." After describing the voting procedure that was to follow his speech, he continued: "principles are eternal, and this has been a contest over principle." He reviewed the declaration of the Congressional Democrats he had written a year before, the organization of the silver forces that had followed, and their successes. "Our silver Democrats went forth from victory unto victory until they are now assembled, not to discuss, not to debate, but to enter up the judgment already rendered by the plain people of this country." Bryan later recalled that "the audience seemed to rise and sit down as one man. At the close of a sentence it would rise and shout, and when I began upon another sentence, the room was as still as church."

He returned to address the gold delegates. "When you come before us and tell us that we are about to disturb your business interests, we reply that you have disturbed our business interests by your course." Bryan offered his own definition of a businessman: "The man who is employed for wages is as much a business man as his employer; the attorney in a country town is as much a business man as the corporation counsel in a great metropolis; the merchant at the cross-roads store is as much a business man as the merchant of New York; the farmer who goes forth in the morning and toils all day— who begins in the spring and toils all summer—and who by the application of brain and muscle to the natural resources of the country creates wealth, is as much a business man as the man who goes upon the board of trade and bets upon the price of grain; the miners who go down a thousand feet into the earth, or climb two thousand feet upon the cliffs, and bring forth from their hiding places the precious metals to be poured into the channels of trade are as much business men as the few financial magnates who, in a back room, corner the money of the world. We come to speak for this broader class of business men."

He waited for the shouting to subside, again denied any animosity toward "those who live upon the Atlantic coast," but claimed to speak for "the pioneers away out there"— pointing to the West—who "are as deserving of the consideration of our party as any people in this country." "Our war is not a war of conquest," he continued, explaining that "we are fighting in the defense of our homes, our families, and posterity. We have petitioned, and our petitions have been disregarded; we have begged, and they have mocked when our calamity came. We beg no longer; we entreat no more; we petition no more. We defy them." Bryan defended the income tax, criticized the Supreme Court for having recently declared it unconstitutional, and refuted several criticisms posed by Senator Hill.

"And now, my friends," he promised, "let me come to the paramount issue," Everyone fell silent to hear his exposition of the money question. "When we have restored the money of the Constitution all other necessary reforms will be accomplished." he began, adding "until this is done there is no other reform that can be accomplished." He characterized the Republican platform as favoring "the maintenance of the gold standard until it can be changed into bimetallism by international agreement." Bryan argued that this provision played into the hands of the Democrats: "If they tell us that the gold standard is a good thing, we shall point to their platform and tell them that their platform pledges the party to get rid of the gold standard and substitute bimetallism. . . . If the gold standard is a good thing, we ought to declare in favor of its retention and not in favor of abandoning it; and if the gold standard is a bad thing why should we wait until other nations are willing to help us let go?"

Bryan next tied the money question to larger concerns, asking whether the Democratic party would take the side of "the idle holders of idle capital" or "the struggling masses." He answered that "the sympathies of the Democratic party, as shown by the platform, are on the side of the struggling masses who have ever been the foundation of the Democratic party. There are two ideas of government. There are those who believe that, if you will only legislate to make the well-to-do prosperous, their prosperity will leak through on those below. The Democratic idea, however, has been that if you legislate to make the masses prosperous, their prosperity will find its way up through every class which rests upon them."

"You come to us and tell us that the great cities are in favor of the gold standard," he continued, "we reply that the great cities rest upon our broad and fertile prairies. Burn down your cities and leave our farms, and your cities will spring up again as if by magic; but destroy our farms and the grass will grow in the streets of every city in the country."

After comparing the silver struggle to that of 1776 and restating some key arguments, Bryan moved to his conclusion. "Having behind us the producing masses of this nation and the world, supported by the commercial interest, the laboring interests, and the toilers everywhere, we will answer their demand for a gold standard by saying to them: You shall not press down upon the brow of labor this crown of thorns." Bryan suggestively raked his fingers down his temples. "You shall not crucify mankind upon a cross of gold." He stretched his arms straight out from his sides as if on a cross and stood silent for a moment, then dropped his arms and took a step back.

The delegates sat in stunned silence as Bryan began to return to the floor. Then the demonstration came, shaking the hall for a half hour. Delegates carried Bryan around the hall on their shoulders, and others came to him to shout their support for the nomination. Bryan's "Cross of Gold" speech achieved instant immortality. John Peter Altgeld, governor of Illinois and a supporter of Bland for the nomination, immediately called it "the greatest speech I have ever listened to," but soon asked his friend Clarence Darrow, "What did he say anyhow?"

The speech achieved its effect as much by the occasion and the style as by the content. The anxious silver delegates knew they had the majority but many were only weakly committed to a candidate. Bryan later described the need of the moment as "to put into words the sentiments of a majority of the delegates." He proved ideal for the task. His voice, a carefully cultivated and powerful instrument, could reach into every part of the great convention hall, an important ability in a day before electronic amplification. Many of his most striking phrases had been tested earlier, when he made speeches across the nation or in Congress. Riding on the train to Chicago, he had spent his time organizing his thoughts in expectation of an opportunity to speak at the convention. Anticipating the arguments his opponents would adduce, he made final plans the night before, summoning all his best metaphors from a thousand rehearsals. On the convention floor, he added a few references to the previous speakers and stood forth as what he later called "the voice of a triumphant majority." The speech immediately transformed Bryan from a presumptuous youngster in the rear ranks of the peripheral candidates into a top contender for the nomination. His performance became the standard example of the ability of an orator to sway a convention. In 1953, a poll of 277 professors of American history or government ranked the "Cross of Gold" speech among the fifty most significant documents in American history.

During the demonstration following the speech, some delegates demanded that the nomination balloting begin immediately, but Bryan refused. Instead, the convention proceeded with its normal order of business, adopted the platform by more than two-thirds margin, and then turned to selecting a presidential candidate. Most pre-convention polls had given the lead to Bland, followed by Horace Boies of Iowa. On the first ballot, Bland led as predicted, but Bryan edged Boies out of second place. Both Bland and Bryan gained on the second ballot, but Bryan gained more than Bland. The pattern repeated itself on the third ballot and Bryan moved into the lead on the fourth ballot. Bland withdrew on the fifth ballot, turning the movement toward Bryan into a stampede and giving him the necessary two-thirds. Telegrams of congratulations rained upon the Bryan hotel suite as silver leaders gathered to discuss the vice-presidential nomination. Bryan refused to designate a choice. On the fifth ballot, the convention nominated Arthur Sewall of Maine, a wealthy shipbuilder and bank president who favored free silver and the income tax. The ticket now showed balance: West and East, lawyer and businessman, youth and experience.

In mid-June, the streets of St. Louis had resounded with enthusiasm for McKinley as Republican convention delegates flouted McKinley badges, hats, and canes. A month later, the streets filled again, this time with whiskered Populists, a few of whom had walked to the convention because they could not afford the train fare. The date for their convention had been set on the assumption that both old parties would reject silver, and that they would reap a bountiful harvest of recruits. Now they faced a distressing dilemma. One horn of the dilemma featured endorsement of Bryan and Sewall, a prospect that meant losing their separate identity as a party and accepting candidates committed to a platform at variance with the Omaha platform at several points; the other horn of the dilemma involved nomination of a separate Populist national ticket on a full-blown Populist platform, thereby dividing the opposition to McKinley and guaranteeing the victory of the gold standard. Threats to bolt compounded the predicament. If the convention nominated Bryan and Sewall, some Southern Populists would walk out; if the delegates chose to nominate their own national ticket, many Western Populists would leave.

The National Silver party, also meeting in St. Louis, provided little assistance to the Populists in resolving their dilemma. With no history as a party and little grass-roots organization, it possessed no real identity beyond the silver issue. The 731 delegates included 528 former Republicans, many of whom held office in silver-mining or farming states. One observer compared the Silver gathering to a Kentucky militia unit: all colonels and no troops. No rancor disturbed their deliberations as they went through the motions of endorsing Bryan and Sewall. Reporters found the meetings to be less a convention than "Bryan hurrah sessions."

In the end, the Populists tried to resolve their dilemma by first asserting their own separate identity as a party, then by endorsing Bryan and uniting the silver forces. The first step to maintain their identity came with the nomination of Tom

Watson for vice-president. Watson yielded to no one in his commitment to the party and in his dislike for the Democrats who had employed fraud on a massive scale to defeat him and his party in Georgia. Many of those who voted for Watson may have believed that the Democrats would withdraw Sewall and put Watson in his place. Senator James K. Jones, Bryan's representative in St. Louis, warned key Populists that Bryan would not drop Sewall, but delegates either ignored the warnings or else believed rampant rumors to the contrary. Having nominated Watson, the convention then approved a platform that reiterated the stands of 1892 and added a call for public works projects to provide employment in times of depression. The platform also sympathized with the Cuban independence movement and opposed disenfranchisement of black voters in the South. A number of these proposals stood in contradiction to the Democratic platform or the sentiments of Democratic party leaders, especially calls for government ownership and the condemnation of black disenfranchisement. Some anti-Fusionists tried to amend the platform to make it even less acceptable to the Democrats, but the convention chairman, William V. Allen (Bryan's fellow Nebraskan), refused to recognize them. Having preserved their identity as a separate party, the Populists then nominated Bryan by the overwhelming vote of 1,042 to 340. Bryan had telegraphed Allen that he would not accept the Populist nomination unless they also nominated Sewall; Allen ignored the telegram and declared Bryan the nominee.

The Populists' call for a public works program for the unemployed reflected the influence of Jacob Coxey, an Ohio Populist who had recently led an army of the unemployed in a march on Washington, demanding jobs. It also reflected the impact of nationwide depression. The depression had begun with the collapse of the Philadelphia and Reading Railroad in the early months of 1893. Other railroads soon followed. New railroad construction ground to a halt, causing steel mills to reduce production. The stock market plunged to record lows in May and continued to fall there-after. By December, companies operating nearly a quarter of the railroad mileage in the country had claimed bank-ruptcy, including all but one of the transcontinental lines; six hundred banks and sixteen thousand businesses had also declared bankruptcy. Estimates of unemployment ranged from one to three million. Chicago reported that one-sixth of its labor force could find no work during the winter of 1893. The complex causes of the depression included over-expansion of railroads in the 1880s, the end of agricultural expansion, a decline in foreign investment (precipitated in part perhaps by the inflationist agitation), and the drain on the Treasury gold reserves caused by the Sherman Silver Purchase Act. Silverites accused Wall Street financiers; gold standard advocates blamed the Sherman Act. Free trade proponents fastened on the McKinley Tariff of 1890 as the cause, while protectionists cited Democratic tampering with that meaure. The APA pointed to the Pope; others to an international conspiracy of Jewish bankers. In 1894, most voters took aim at the party in power. Massive Democratic losses that year reflected the same tendency to blame Cleve-land, which assisted the silver Democrats in their drive to take control of their party.

McKinley's campaign organizers gave due attention to the depression as they worked the two longstanding Republican themes of prosperity and patriotism. "Prosperity" involved blaming Cleveland and the Democrats for the depression and arguing that the solution could only come through a protective tariff and "sound money," i.e., the gold standard. Bryan's silver policy, McKinley argued, would bring inflation and prove harmful to all; the Republican policy of protec-tion would aid manufacturers, as well as their employees, who enjoyed the highest wages in the world. "Patriotism" took the form of a nationalistic appeal for unity against Democratic efforts to divide the country by class and section.

Billed as "the advance agent of prosperity," McKinley followed the traditional practice of presidential candidates by staying home, in Canton, Ohio, and allowing his party to carry the campaign to the voters. Hanna efficiently transformed his preconvention organization into a structure for winning in November. Just as the convention had run like clockwork, so the campaign ticked away in the same fashion. The Republicans wrote off the South and much of the West. They assumed that the East would be theirs with minimal effort, but they knew that the Middle West would be the crucial battle ground.

The McKinley campaign featured extensive organization and ample funding. Hanna employed old-line political techniques of polling and voter mobilization, but added the new methods of advertising. The pamphlets, posters, buttons, and other campaign gewgaws that poured from McKinley headquarters led Theodore Roosevelt to snort that Hanna "advertised McKinley as if he were a patent medicine." The Republican campaign relied heavily on distributing materials, especially pamphlets of every sort, aimed at almost every conceivable audience, from bicyclists to Germans. Materials left the Chicago campaign headquarters in boxcar lots. By the end of the campaign, 250 million items had gone out, equivalent to eighteen for every vote cast in November. Such lavish distributions required formidable financing. Hanna played on Eastern businessmen's fears of Bryan—it did not take much—to collect a campaign fund he acknowledged at nearly four million dollars, more than double the previous record for presidential campaigns. Total McKinley campaign expenditures—national, state, and local—reached ten to sixteen million dollars. Donations came in large sums. Standard Oil and J. P. Morgan each gave a quarter million, railroad companies contributed $174,000, and Chicago meat-packing companies kicked in $40,000.

Bryan conducted his entire campaign with only about $300,000. Local and state committees may have collected and spent a similar amount. The *New York Journal* raised

$40,000, of which $15,000 came from the publisher, William Randolph Hearst. A few large contributions came from western mining interests, but all mining interests together gave less than Standard Oil's contribution to McKinley. The Bryan forces distributed ten million campaign speeches and pamphlets and over a hundred thousand copies of *Coin's Financial School,* but they could not possibly match the unlimited quantities of materials, the degree of organization, and the depth of financial support which Hanna commanded. Where the McKinley campaign resembled precision clockwork, Bryan's effort exhibited a distinctly amateurish appearance. In the end, his most important campaign asset proved to be the instrument which won him the nomination—his voice.

Between his nomination and election day, Bryan traveled 18,000 miles by train, visited 26 states and more than 250 cities, and addressed as many as five million people. He once delivered thirty speeches during twenty-four hours; the total number of Bryan speeches during the campaign reached three thousand. In addition to scheduled speeches, he spoke virtually every time the train stopped. Announcement that his train would come through town invariably brought a crowd to the station, even in the middle of the night. Mary accompanied him for much of the campaign.

His first cross-country trip of the campaign, in early August, took him to New York City, which he described to Lincoln neighbors as being "in the heart of what now seems to be the enemy's country." There he gave a most important speech. So that Eastern newspapers would report the speech accurately, he read it, instead of speaking extemporaneously. He intended to present a clear, logical, conservative exposition of bimetallism, and thereby to counter those press accounts picturing him as a dangerous rabble-rouser. He knew that reading the speech would dull its effect; he later wrote that "it was necessary to make the speech as brief as possible because the crime of reading a speech increases in heinousness in proportion to its length." While he knew the virtues of brevity, especially when the temperature stood above 90°, he still took two hours to finish the speech. By then, whole sections of the hall stood vacant.

Bryan's cool reception in New York marked the occasion as unusual. Most of his public appearances drew throngs, some committed, some only curious. "Sixteen-to-one," Bryan's proposed ratio for silver coinage, prompted local admirers to greet him with a bouquet of sixteen white flowers and one yellow, or to escort him with sixteen young women dressed in white and one in yellow. Others showered him with curios and good luck symbols. More than seven hundred babies were named for Bryan during the year, including three sets of triplets, each named "William," "Jennings," and "Bryan."

Bryan's campaign encountered severe logistical problems. Until late September, he had to do most of his preparations while en route. He traveled on regularly scheduled trains and sometimes carried his own bags and walked from the depot. Eventually he acquired assistance with such details; in early October the Democratic National Committee arranged a private railroad car. But local arrangements remained only as good as the committees that made them. Larger problems arose in dealing with the Populists. Although Bryan later insisted that "under the conditions then existing two Vice-Presidential candidates were better than one," Watson soon became an irritant. After Bryan repeatedly announced his confidence in Sewall, Watson suggested that fusion meant "that we play Jonah while they play whale." In most states, the Bryan-Sewall ticket went on the ballot, and Populists received only modest recognition. When the Georgia Populist committee withdrew Watson's name from the ballot in his own state, he advised a crowd, "There are two tickets you can vote—for Bryan and Sewall, or for McKinley and Hobart; or if you can't stand either you can stay away from the election next Tuesday and not vote at all."

But most Populists, especially in the West, put on the
Bryan harness and toiled for his cause. He also found important support from leaders of organized labor, especially
officers of the Knights of Labor, the United Mine Workers,
and the Chicago Building Trades Council. Eugene V. Debs,
leader of the Pullman strike of 1894, gave Bryan his blessing. Bryan must have hoped that his presidential campaign
would reproduce, on a national scale, the coalition that had
proven victorious in Nebraska in the 1894 gubernatorial
campaign. He had then united Populists with most Democrats, especially Catholics who feared the political power of
the APA. He could cite a strong and impressive record of
opposition to the APA; his record against prohibition should
have lost him no support among those who liked their beer.
If he could hold the ethnic core of the Middle Western
Democratic party, *if* he could attract economically distressed
farmers and workers, *if* southern Democrats and Populists
could set aside local differences during the campaign, *if* the
western mining states would deliver votes as anticipated,
then he would win. Early in October, a survey by the *New
York Herald* indicated that Bryan held 237 electoral votes, a
clear majority.

Early Republican campaign polls revealed that McKinley
might have difficulty carrying key Middle Western states,
even his own Ohio. Much of the paper blizzard originating
from his Chicago headquarters focused on this crucial territory. In early September, a group of Democrats met in Indianapolis and nominated two Civil War generals, one from each
side, to run as candidates of the National Democratic party,
usually called the Gold Democrats. Their platform praised
Cleveland and gold. Although most of the funding for this
splinter party came from the East, their campaign centered in
the Middle West. The Gold Democrats had no thought of
winning a single state; they hoped instead to persuade Democratic voters of the dangers of silver coinage and to draw votes
from Bryan. By late October, the Gold Democrats' candidate

for president told a gathering in Missouri that he would find no fault with them if they voted for McKinley. A few weeks before the end of the campaign, Republican headquarters in Chicago dispatched 1,400 speakers to states still in doubt. Hanna sprung his most audacious campaign tactic in the last week of October: he proclaimed a day to display the flag as a symbol of support for McKinley. Bryan responded by asking his supporters to fly the flag, but as a symbol of patriotism, not party. Bryan's rejoinder came late; the McKinley campaign moved into its final days tightly wrapped in the flag.

During the closing month of the campaign, Bryan devoted much of his time to the Middle West, especially Illinois, Indiana, Michigan, and Ohio, but he proved unable to hold the ethnic core of his party there. In 1894, the Nebraska fusion campaign had been blessed with a rabidly anti-Catholic Republican opponent. By contrast, the APA had marked McKinley before the Republican convention as the most unacceptable Republican seeking the nomination. McKinley condemned the secret order; by election day, he benefited both from some support among Catholics (attracted either by his treatment of economic issues or by his condemnation of the APA) and from the resigned APA attitude that the Republican ticket was preferable to the Democratic. McKinley could also point to support from a few labor leaders. Both the gold standard and McKinley's refusal to associate himself with prohibition sentiment helped his cause among German voters; one survey indicated that McKinley had the support of 503 of the nation's 581 German language newspapers. His approach was so broad that it could attract both a Catholic archbishop and the APA, prohibitionists and saloonkeepers, unionists and adamantly anti-union employers.

Election day saw four of every five eligible voters troop to the polls, a level of participation never since matched. In the critical Middle Western states—Iowa, Illinois, Indiana, Ohio, Michigan—turnouts of eligible voters reached 95 percent and more. After the polls closed, voters gathered in huge crowds outside newspaper offices, on courthouse lawns, or in meeting halls, to await the result. Bryan had garnered almost 6.5 million votes, nearly a million more than any previous presidential candidate had ever won. But McKinley got even more, 7.1 million. McKinley won 23 states and 271 electoral votes, Bryan took 22 states and 176 electoral votes. The Republicans carried a solid East and every closely contested Middle Western state, as well as four border states. Bryan took the South and most of the West.

Bryan quickly calculated that if 19,436 voters in six states had switched from McKinley to himself, he would have won. He also pointed to widespread coercion of voters throughout the East and Middle West. Businessmen made orders to manufacturers contingent upon a McKinley victory; some companies told their workers to return to work after election day if McKinley won, but to stay home if Bryan were elected. Loan companies offered farmers five-year extensions on their loans at low interest if McKinley won. Bryan's supporters claimed outright fraud as well; in key states, some areas recorded more votes than there were eligible voters. Several supporters claimed that an honest election would have put Bryan in the White House; one Bryan confidant indicated that Bryan agreed with this view.

McKinley's victory arose from the urban industrial core of the nation. The states he carried included the lion's share of manufacturing, commerce, and finance. Of the twenty largest cities in the nation, Bryan won a majority only in New Orleans. His advocacy of inflation held little appeal to those who lived in cities. As one Kansas editor put it, "McKinley won because the Republicans had persuaded the middle class, almost to a man, that a threat to the gold standard was a threat to their prosperity." McKinley was also able to make major gains among German voters. The Middle West held high concentrations of German stock voters; many of them moved from the Democrats to the party of the gold standard. Bryan retained the loyalty of most Irish Democrats, whether in the Middle West or in the East. In Kentucky, the Gold Democratic presidential ticket drew enough votes from Bryan to throw that state to McKinley. Bryan pitched his campaign to debtors and farmers and hoped for the support of urban labor and traditional Democrats. In the end, his "paramount issue" failed to produce the response induced by McKinley's appeals for "honest money" and "national honor."

Bryan had broken with one precedent by taking his case directly to the people. He created another precedent by cabling his congratulations to McKinley. In defeat, Bryan received an avalanche of letters and telegrams from well-wishers. He spent no time in misgiving or remorse. Within a few weeks of election day, Mary wrote to Dr. Jones in Jacksonville that "Will does not feel discouraged—he is working very hard—getting material together for our book about the campaign." The book, *The First Battle,* sold 200,000 copies within nine months. In its title and in the message issued to his supporters, Bryan made clear that the campaign would continue. "If we are right," Bryan promised, "we shall yet triumph."

Despite Bryan's optimism about the future, McKinley's victory inaugurated a generation of Republican dominance of American politics. From 1896 through 1928, the GOP won seven out of nine presidential elections, usually held sizable majorities in both houses of Congress, and typically claimed more than half the nation's governors. From his sixteenth year to his thirty-sixth, Bryan had lived in a closely competitive political system with neither party holding a strong advantage. He was to live his final twenty-nine years in a system in which his party usually found itself in the role of critic rather than initiator. The role suited Bryan.

I V

Crusade against Imperialism

ALTHOUGH BRYAN'S APPEAL to traditional Democrats and the "laboring masses" failed to carry him to the
White House in 1896, he could take some consolation in the
success of the coalition in Nebraska. He spent the day before
the election on a final swing through his own state, and his
campaign struck a strong response where the voters knew
him best. Silas Holcomb won reelection by a larger majority
than in 1894, leading even Bryan. The Fusion ticket secured
all state-wide offices, most Congressional seats, and lopsided
majorities in the legislature. Similar Fusion victories occurred nearby in Kansas and South Dakota. Bryan began to
plan for the next presidential campaign and left his law
partnership with Adolphus Talbot in order to devote his full
energies to that task. He donated half the royalties from *The
First Battle* to the silver parties; the remaining royalties and
his income from speaking engagements proved sufficient to
support his family. Life in the household on D Street began
to take on a more predictable pattern.

Grace, the youngest child, may have been thinking of this
time when she recalled that "the morning family prayer . . .
is my earliest remembrance of my parents. Father read from
the Bible; the family then gathered around the piano to
unite in singing several stirring hymns, the accompani-
ment . . . played by Mother. A prayer by either Father or my
maternal grandfather, John Baird, closed our morning
family worship." She also described Bryan's morning prayer

as "the sunlight of my father's spiritual life." Bryan's morning meditations, even in this time of comparative calm, often
took place in a railroad car or hotel room, for his lecture
calendar rapidly filled with engagements around the nation.

When not on the lecture circuit, W.J. (as he signed his

Mary Baird Bryan visiting Colonel William Jennings Bryan while
the 3d Nebraska Volunteer Infantry waited for action at Camp
Cuba Libre, Florida, 1898. (Photograph courtesy of the Nebraska
State Historical Society.)

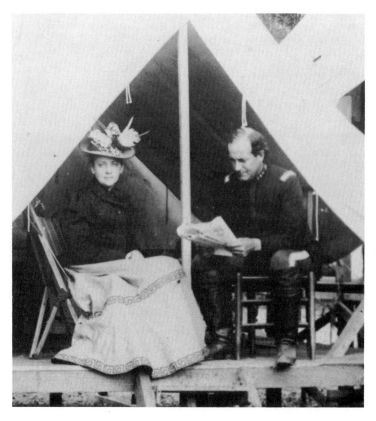

name and increasingly came to be called) and Mary presided over a large household. It was nearly as large as that in which Bryan had grown up. Mary's mother and W.J.'s mother had died without seeing his nomination for president, but the Bryan home in Lincoln held Mary's father, now blind, the three children, and also Dan Bride, born in Ireland, who came to work for Bryan during the years in Congress and continued to do whatever was necessary for the next quarter-century. In 1898, a young Japanese lad, Yachichiro Yamashita, appeared on the doorstep, "his valise in hand," Mary recalled, and asked to live with and be educated by the Bryans. The Bryans took him in, at first for the night, but eventually for five years, until he graduated from the University. When Bryan worked at home, he preferred his study, surrounded by his books and mementos of his campaigns. In the center of the room stood a large two-sided desk, so that W.J. and Mary might work together. Mary sometimes accompanied W.J. on his trips; she employed help for the house and could leave the children without worrying. When in Lincoln, she busied herself with a variety of civic activities, especially those connected with the University. She also enjoyed bicycling and swimming.

In 1897, in addition to his lecturing, Bryan had to face the annual Nebraska political conventions and election. The occasion was to prove a test of the coalition that had carried the state so convincingly in 1896. Fusion candidates swept every state-wide office, confirming the viability of Bryan's political base. All three Fusion party platforms also included expressions of sympathy for Cuban independence.

When revolution broke out in Cuba in 1895, the Spanish authorities responded with repression so brutal as to produce severe suffering among insurgents and noninsurgents alike. Governor Holcomb promptly expressed hope for the success of the insurrection and urged Americans to lend moral and material aid. The 1896 national platforms of both Democrats and Populists sympathized with the insurgents;

the Populists had called for recognition of them. During the Fifty-fifth Congress, six silverite senators introduced resolutions urging action on the Cuban situation; Senator Allen alone introduced four. Most members of Bryan's faction of the Democratic party and most Populists deeply sympathized with the struggles of the Cubans to achieve independence from Spain. McKinley's cautious response to the Cuban liberation effort led some Fusion leaders to condemn him for callousness in the face of the suffering of the island people. Bryan refused to criticize McKinley's course, recommending instead that the nation support the president's efforts to avoid war.

On April 11, 1898, when McKinley finally asked Congress for authority to intervene, Bryan expressed caution. "War is a terrible thing," he warned, "and cannot be defended except as a means to an end." The only proper end, in Bryan's view, was a humanitarian goal, in this case, ending the mistreatment of the Cubans and assisting them to secure independence. Bryan urged his supporters on Capitol Hill to extend immediate diplomatic recognition to the Cuban revolutionary government. This effort failed on a near straight party vote in the House of Representatives. The silver forces did secure a resolution, written by Senator Teller, disclaiming any intention of exercising permanent authority over Cuba or its people. The resolutions authorizing intervention, passed on April 20, led Spain to declare war on April 24. Congress voted a declaration of war on April 25. On that same day, Bryan cabled the president, offering his services in whatever capacity should prove most appropriate. Bryan's offer lay on McKinley's desk when, on May 1, Commodore George Dewey took his naval squadron into Manila harbor; he destroyed the Spanish fleet stationed there, then waited for troops to extend operations to the land. Most Americans had their attention focused on Cuba and learned with surprise of Dewey's actions halfway around the globe.

When Bryan received no response from the War Department or the president by mid-May, he enlisted as a volunteer; Holcomb soon named him colonel of the Third Nebraska Volunteer Regiment. Many of Bryan's Fusion allies objected to his enlistment, Allen arguing that it "would dignify the war beyond its merit." Before the regiment went on active duty, Bryan delivered a farewell speech; in it, he linked the surprise people felt over the Dewey victory with the fear that the war, undertaken for humanity, might become "a war of conquest" aimed at acquisition of territory. "Our guns destroyed a Spanish fleet," he said, but then asked, "can they destroy the self-evident truth, that governments derive their just powers, not from superior force, but from the consent of the governed?" He then made no more political speeches, announcing that he had "military lockjaw" until he left uniform.

Bryan had little experience either with the military or with leadership of a large body of men, and he conducted his colonelcy with minimum amount of military spit and polish. Bryan drew few distinctions between officers and enlisted men, preferring to entrust some decisions to a vote of his unit. He left most military matters to Victor Vifquain, his lieutenant colonel. Vifquain, a long-time Nebraska Democrat, had graduated from a military academy in his native Belgium before coming to the United States; he had been breveted brigadier general during the Civil War. The regiment arrived in Florida, in mid-July, to await assignment to Cuba. They were still waiting two months later, their numbers devastated by typhoid and other sicknesses. Rumors flourished that the administration intended to keep Bryan's unit in service but out of action. Such a tactic would deny Bryan any military laurels and simultaneously keep him out of the fall political campaigns. In late September, Bryan, Holcomb, and Allen went to Washington to see McKinley and to ask that the unit be mustered out. By then the fighting had been over for two months, the armistice in effect for one. Bryan argued that the war had changed course and that those who had volunteered to assist the Cubans ought to be sent home. "They did not volunteer to attempt to subjugate other peoples, or establish United States sovereignty elsewhere," Bryan lectured the president. McKinley refused, telling him such a request must go through proper channels.

Bryan soon came down with typhoid himself, losing all the weight he had put on over six years of political banquets and hotel meals. As he suffered in Florida, the fall election campaign came and went. While some Fusionists in the Middle West argued against the acquisition of overseas possessions, they reached no party consensus. Republican newspapers asked, "Will you vote for Spain?" and made clear their view that Spain would benefit from a vote for Fusion candidates. Voting Republican, they argued, would tell Spain that the American people supported McKinley's course. Nonetheless, Fusion carried the state-wide offices in Nebraska and four Congressional seats; the legislature, however, went to the Republicans. The loss of the legislature in Nebraska endangered Senator Allen, for his term was to expire in 1899. Fusion campaigns in other states met less success than in Nebraska. When Bryan enlisted, one of his supporters protested to Mary that W.J. could not "be spared from the mighty contest now waging in favor of the rights of the people." From the results in the Nebraska legislature and in other states, it began to appear that this evaluation had been correct. Bryan fretted in Florida, impatiently waiting for some rationale to return to civilian life. When the Paris peace treaty was signed in December, Bryan promptly resigned his commission and hurried to Washington.

The Treaty of Paris bore out Bryan's worst fears. Spain surrendered all claim to Cuba and gave the United States title to the Philippines, Puerto Rico, Guam, and several small Caribbean islands. The treaty promised free exercise of religion to the inhabitants of new territories, but left their civil and political rights for Congressional determination. Every previous treaty by which the United States had acquired territory had stipulated that those inhabitants who had been citizens of the other nation immediately gained full rights as American citizens. Nor did the Treaty of Paris contain any promise of eventual statehood for the acquisitions; all previous treaties except that for the purchase of Alaska had promised statehood when the territories reached sufficient population. Bryan and his party swiftly applied a label to this new approach to territorial acquisition: imperialism.

Bryan spoke out strongly against imperialism, arguing that administration of the Philippines as a possession would violate the most fundamental concept of the nation, that of self-government. Most silverites in Congress shared similar fears. Senator Richard Pettigrew, a Silver Republican from South Dakota, had long since concluded that "this is not a patriotic war," but "a war of plundering and spoils." Yet Bryan and Pettigrew disagreed on tactics. Pettigrew and a number of others preferred to vote down the Treaty of Paris in order to prevent acquisition of the Philippines. Bryan favored approval of the treaty. He wanted the war to come to an official end, so that those who had volunteered might be mustered out and sent home. He also worried—probably without cause—that rejection of the treaty would allow for resumption of hostilities. He feared as well for the future of the Philippines. If the United States refused to accept them, they might remain colonial subjects of Spain or fall into the clutches of another imperial power. Bryan wanted to approve the treaty in order to sever the islands from Spain, then quickly grant them independence and guarantee it by action of Congress. He later explained that he believed it easier "to persuade the American people to promise independence to the Filipinos . . . than to continue war and force Spain to recognize a republic of the Philippines."

The Senate voted on the Treaty of Paris in early February 1899. Approval required a two-thirds majority. Republicans stood nearly unanimously in favor of it. Despite Bryan's efforts to persuade his party to support the treaty, two-thirds of the Democrats voted against it. He had somewhat better success in convincing third-party silverites; Populists, Silver Republicans, and Silver party members split seven in favor, three opposed. Bryan's urgings probably swung the votes of two senators. Had those two changed sides, they would have defeated the treaty.

Bryan's plan for Philippine independence took form in a Senate resolution introduced by Senator Augustus Bacon of Georgia. The Bacon Resolution came to a vote less than a week after the approval of the treaty; it produced a tie vote with Republicans mostly against and Democrats strongly in favor. Vice-President Hobart broke the tie by voting against. To the end of his life, Bryan never doubted that his support for the treaty had been correct. He believed his course had placed the decision for Philippine independence with the American people rather than with Spain or any other power. He always trusted the people to make the right decision, eventually if not initially. Defeat in the Senate in February 1899 only meant he had one more great issue to take to the people in the rapidly approaching presidential contest.

By 1899, most Democrats, Populists, and Silver Republicans shared Bryan's view that acquisition of the Philippines violated American commitments to self-government. He took a somewhat different view of the acquisition of Puerto Rico. Bryan thought that Puerto Ricans would probably vote to be annexed to the United States, and he favored giving them the opportunity. If they voted against annexation, he favored independence. Bryan saw no significant support for annexation among Filipinos; during the quarter-century before Dewey destroyed the Spanish fleet, the islands had witnessed repeated efforts to throw off Spanish authority. By the time American troops arrived in Manila, Filipino rebels had proclaimed their independence, taken control over much of the islands, and established a provisional government. The McKinley administration refused to recognize this government. Instead, it announced that Filipinos would have to "accept the supremacy of the United States" if they wished to be eligible for positions of authority. In early February, as the Senate vote on the Treaty of Paris approached, fighting broke out between American troops and those of the Filipino provisional government.

In his efforts to make imperialism the focus of the 1900 presidential campaign, Bryan found some unlikely allies. Cleveland and most other prominent gold Democrats opposed the acquisitions. Some Republicans opposed the majority of their party, but very few allowed their beliefs to lead them into prominent roles in the campaign. A number of well-known reformers, intellectuals, and writers spoke out strongly, among them Mark Twain, William Dean Howells, and Carl Schurz. Among business leaders, only Andrew Carnegie devoted much energy to the cause. Samuel Gompers, president of the American Federation of Labor, made known his opposition, but few labor leaders joined in any extended effort.

The arguments posed by this diverse anti-imperialist crew ranged as widely as their backgrounds. Many joined in arguing that imperialism violated democratic concepts of self-government, and that the constitution nowhere allowed for the acquisition of possessions not intended to become states. Some Populists feared that imperialism would necessitate the creation of a large standing army and navy, which would increase taxes and pose a danger to liberty. William Greene, a Fusion congressman from western Nebraska, argued in 1899 that "the great capitalists" of the nation favored a large standing army to use for "suppressing laboring men." Some anti-imperialists—North and South alike—adduced racist arguments. Carl Schurz, a well-known reformer and a Republican, argued that only persons from northern Europe had shown historical capacity for self-government, and that those peoples had also shown an inability to live in the tropics; therefore, he reasoned, acquisition of tropical territories would inevitably involve the nation in denying self-government to the inhabitants. One Nebraska Populist saw the war as a political ploy, designed to distract people from the money question and to provide McKinley with a mantle of statesmanship.

Bryan seems to have used the Nebraska state campaign of 1899 as a prototype for his 1900 presidential bid. He prepared a volume of essays and articles under the title *Republic or Empire?* and included contributions by leading Democrats, Populists, and Silver Republicans. Other publications soon appeared, including one by W. H. "Coin" Harvey. Under Bryan's direction, the Nebraska Fusion parties drafted state platforms that condemned imperial expansion and militarism. The Democratic platform condemned "the administrative policy which has converted a war for humanity into a war of conquest," demanded that the people of the Philippines be given immediate assurance of independence and protection from outside interference, and denounced "militarism." The language of the Populist platform was nearly identical.

Bryan and his followers made anti-imperialism the keynote of the entire 1899 state campaign. To support the ticket, they brought into the state a host of nationally known silver leaders, including Harvey, Altgeld, James B. Weaver, Charles Towne, a Silver Republican congressman from Minnesota, and James H. "Cyclone" Davis, the Texas Populist. Fusion newspapers condemned administration policies in the Philippines, predicted dire consequences for imperial commitment, and held up the Fusionists as the defenders of American honor and integrity. The Nebraska campaign ended in a Fusion sweep of all major offices. This trial-run of anti-imperialism as a campaign issue seemed to indicate that it had a powerful appeal. Fusion celebrations of their success soon came to a halt, however, because of squabbling over a vacant Senate seat. The Republican legislature had chosen a successor to Allen, but the senator-elect died in December 1899. Populist Governor William Poynter eventu-

ally reappointed Allen, but not before a flurry of controversy erupted. Several Democrats, including *World-Herald*
publisher Gilbert Hitchcock, sought the prize. Bryan made
few friends by first keeping still, then finally intervening on
Allen's behalf.

The Bryan family spent the winter of 1899–1900 in
Texas, primarily because of Grace's poor health. The move
did not slow Bryan's planning for the coming campaign.
Four years earlier, few observers had given him much of a
chance for the nomination. In 1900, his renomination was a
foregone conclusion; no other candidates entered the field.
At least one close adviser urged him not to seek the nomination, suggesting that McKinley would almost surely be re-
elected and that Bryan overestimated imperialism as an issue. Bryan brushed aside such arguments with the statement
that it would be his duty to accept the nomination if the
convention offered it. When the Nebraska Democrats chose
their convention delegates in late March, the platform spoke
to three issues Bryan considered primary: "an unceasing
warfare against all the trusts," the restoration of silver coinage at 16 to 1, and opposition to imperialism and militarism.

The first party convention of the year, that of the Populists,
met in May. In 1896, they had convened after the two major
parties, hoping to gain dissidents from them. By 1900, the
party had splintered and the branch that gathered in Sioux
Falls, South Dakota, hoped to lead the way by nominating
Bryan and choosing a vice-presidential candidate before the
Democrats met. Their platform forecast the positions that the
Democrats were likely to adopt, and they chose Charles
Towne, a leading Silver Republican, for vice-president. In
contrast to the heated deliberations of four years before, few
Populists at Sioux Falls disputed the wisdom of nominating a
Democrat and a Silver Republican. Another Populist conven-
tion met simultaneously in Cincinnati, refused to accept
Bryan, and nominated Wharton Barker, a wealthy Easterner.
This anti-Fusion faction, called the Middle-of-the-Road Pop-

ulists, moved in much the same direction that Gold Democrats had taken in 1896—intentionally splitting off a few votes
that otherwise would have gone to Bryan.

As an announced candidate for the nomination, Bryan
followed tradition and stayed away from the Democratic
convention in Kansas City, Missouri, but he maintained close
contact with developments there. He came under heavy
pressure to back down on the silver issue. Delegates urged
that the platform omit any mention of silver, but instead
reaffirm the 1896 platform in general. Bryan stood adamant, insisting that full support for his issues was a prereq-
uisite for his acceptance of the nomination. He got the platform he desired, won the nomination without opposition,
and allowed the convention to choose his running mate. Although the Populists and Silver Republicans—and perhaps
Bryan as well—hoped for Towne, the Democrats gave the
place to former vice-president Adlai Stevenson of Illinois.
The Silver Republicans, also meeting in Kansas City, eventually accepted Stevenson too. When Towne declined the Populist nomination, they also took Stevenson in his place.
There was to be no repetition of the embarrassment Watson
caused in 1896.

The 1900 campaign lacked more than the embarrassment
the Populist vice-presidential candidate caused in 1896. It
also lacked the enthusiasm Populist and Silver Republicans
had generated that year. Both parties had declined in the
four-year interim, although both still claimed offices in a
number of states. In the South, Populists held on only where
they had coalesced with Republicans. In the Rocky Mountain
West, the leadership of the silver cause had shifted almost
entirely to Silver Republicans; in many areas the Populist
party withered. Only in the western Middle West did the
Populists possess anything like their old vigor; even there
they had done poorly in the 1898 elections. Bryan also lost
supporters among Populists who found the Republican imperial policy attractive. Former Kansas Senator William A.

Peffer converted to McKinley, arguing that the acquisition of the Philippines provided "some outlet for the surplus of things we have to spare," thus reducing the specter of "lack of employment for the people."

Although the 1900 campaign lacked the fire the Populists had supplied in 1896, Bryan was pleased with the support of some Gold Democrats. Many conservative Democrats found McKinley's acquisition of the Philippines more troublesome than Bryan's continued insistence on free coinage of silver at 16 to 1. They returned to their party and a few even took to the campaign trail, speaking out against imperialism and McKinley. Other Gold Democrats, even those active in anti-imperialist organizations, simply sat out the campaign and glumly voted for McKinley as the lesser of two evils. "I am going to shut my eyes," J. Sterling Morton wrote to Cleveland, "hold my nose, vote, go home, and disinfect myself."

McKinley received a triumphal renomination at his party's convention in Philadelphia. The platform spoke with pride of the Republicans' "unsurpassed record of achievement," and called McKinley "the true American patriot and the upright statesman." The only uncertainty of the convention came over the nomination of the vice-presidential candidate. Garret Hobart, McKinley's choice of 1896, died in 1899, and McKinley watched a growing boom in Theodore Roosevelt's popularity. Roosevelt had parlayed a brief war record into the status of a hero. Serving only three and a half months—a bit more than half Bryan's service time—Roosevelt garnered considerable press attention for his leadership of a cavalry unit, the Rough Riders. He took part in one dramatic assault, then resigned his commission and returned to New York state to run for governor. Throughout the 1899 campaign, he toured the country for Republican candidates, drawing large crowds everywhere he went. Hanna disliked Roosevelt and tried to convince McKinley to oppose him. McKinley tried to persuade a few supporters to enter the vice-presidential contest, but when no one seemed interested, he left the matter to the convention. After Roosevelt took the nomination, Hanna wrote to his leader in Canton that "your *duty* to the country is to *live* for *four* years from next March."

The nomination of Roosevelt for vice-president gave the Republican ticket a magnetic, energetic speaker with a strong commitment to "expansion"; Republicans avoided the term "imperialism." Roosevelt had long been among leading Republicans urging acquisition of overseas possessions. With respect to the Philippines, the Republican platform had spoken of "the high duty of the Government to maintain its authority, to put down armed insurrection and to confer the blessings of liberty and civilization upon all the rescued peoples." Roosevelt carried the message throughout the campaign. The administration would offer no commitment on the future of the Philippines until the insurrection ended; any other course might be interpreted as weakness. Republican campaigners charged that Bryan's talk of independence for the Philippines only encouraged the insurgents, prolonged the war, and cost more American lives. Some Republican campaigners also pointed to the benefits of acquiring the islands, focusing upon the importance of Manila Bay for naval operations and upon commercial expansion. One GOP pamphlet forecast a great growth of the trans-Pacific trade and showed Manila as the center of "the Orient," a market center for eight hundred million people.

While Republicans gave due attention to rebutting Democratic charges regarding acquisition of the Philippines, much of the GOP campaign concentrated on other issues. McKinley, Hanna, and other planners believed that the weakest part of Bryan's campaign was his insistence on silver coinage. During the four years after 1896, the money supply had expanded as a result of new gold discoveries and new technologies. The commercial price for silver had dropped to the equivalent of 22 to 1; when Bryan insisted that the platform include 16 to 1, he handed McKinley an

immediate advantage. Republican campaign pronounce-
ments scored the silver issue again and again, labeling
Bryan a "menace to labor and industry."

The most prominent Republican campaign theme was
prosperity. McKinley took the "Full Dinner Pail" as his symbol to indicate the contrast between the depression years of
Cleveland and the Democrats and the more prosperous
years since his election. Cartoons contrasted "Democratic
Hard Times" and "Republican Good Times." Campaign
pamphlets carried the "full dinner pail" argument to the
farmer, arguing that "opening of the mills to American labor" had caused increased demand for farm products and
higher prices. "A full dinner pail," Republicans claimed,
"causes good prices." When Democrats attacked the trusts,
McKinley simply agreed that "dangerous conspiracies
against the public good . . . should be made the subject of
prohibitory or penal legislation."

Not only did McKinley strategists trumpet the traditional
Republican claim as the party of prosperity, but they also
maintained their party's ability to wrap itself in the flag and
to claim a monopoly on patriotism. While Democrats outlined abstract concepts of the right to self-government, Republicans asked rhetorically who would dare to lower the
flag where it waved over American dead. Faced with armed
opposition to American sovereignty in the Philippines, they
blamed Bryan and the Democrats for its continuation. Colonel Bryan's regiment had never been close to action, but
Colonel Roosevelt had seen action long enough for him to
boast that "I killed a Spaniard with my own hand."

Hanna ran McKinley's campaign again, but the massive
fund raising of 1896 seemed less necessary. The Republicans
spent perhaps $5 million, about half of it from the national
headquarters, with donations largely from the same sources
as in 1896. Carnegie would give nothing to the party responsible for acquisition of the Philippines, but other businessmen
felt no such compunctions. Hanna even made some refunds

when the campaign was over. The campaign headquarters sent out 125 million documents and 21 million postcards. Six hundred speakers appeared on their payroll; by the end of the campaign, Republican speakers were delivering seven thousand speeches each day. Hanna and Roosevelt shared top billing, both delivering scores of speeches across the nation. The former Rough Rider often spoke with his khaki cavalry hat clamped on his head.

Bryan again carried the largest burden of his campaign. He received only two sizable contributions, both from western mining magnates, one of $50,000, the other of $23,000. (Hanna was able to *refund* $50,000 to Standard Oil at the end of the campaign.) In all, the Democrats raised only a half million dollars, a tenth of the Republican war chest. The role of underdog came as no shock to Bryan, however. He had thoroughly rehearsed the part in 1896. A few other able speakers took to the campaign trail with him, but they could be paid no more than expenses. Bryan concentrated on the states he considered crucial to victory—the Corn Belt states and New York, New Jersey, Maryland, and West Virginia. He set a new record on October 30, by giving 32 speeches on that day, and he often put in seventeen-hour days. Even so, the Republicans outdid the Bryan campaign in speaking. Roosevelt traveled 21,000 miles to Bryan's 19,000 and gave 673 speeches to Bryan's 546.

Bryan sounded the keynote of his campaign in his first major address. For the location, he chose Indianapolis, center of a state vital to his success and one he almost carried four years earlier. Nearly fifty thousand people heard him define the contest as "between Democracy on the one hand and plutocracy on the other." He touched quickly on the money question, briefly scored the trusts, then devoted nearly the entire speech to imperialism. He denied that his speeches or those of other anti-imperialists gave encouragement to Filipino rebels. The insurgents, he argued, needed no encouragement from any living Americans for they could

find ample inspiration from such Americans as Patrick
Henry and Thomas Jefferson. Furthermore, "it was God
himself who placed in every human heart the love of liberty." Bryan differentiated between imperialism and previous expansion, then pointed to the dangers of imperialism
and militarism. A large standing army, he feared, "will inevitably change the ideals of the people and turn the thoughts
of our young men from the arts of peace to the science of
war." Denying Republican claims that Filipinos could not
govern themselves, Bryan stated a principle: "Once admit
that some people are capable of self-government and that
others are not and that the capable people have a right to
seize upon and govern the incapable, and you make force—
brute force—the only foundation of government and invite
the reign of a despot." He acknowledged that some Americans hoped to educate the inhabitants of the Philippines, but
pointed ironically to the dangers of doing so: "We dare not
educate them, lest they learn to read the Declaration of Independence and Constitution of the United States." He
listed all the major justifications for acquisition, and rebutted
them. Bryan read this address, as he had read his New York
City speech in 1896. The purposes were similar: a clear,
logical, rational exposition of the most significant issue of
the campaign. Silver remained written into the platform, but
Bryan sought to make the campaign revolve around foreign
policy.

Everywhere Bryan traveled, he met large, enthusiastic
crowds, even in New York, now no longer "the enemy's
country." Bryan reserved a number of crucial appearances
for Nebraska. The Republicans sent leading orators there,
including Roosevelt and Hanna. The stakes in Bryan's home
state amounted to more than just its eight electoral votes:
Bryan hoped to avoid the embarrassment of losing his own
state, and the Fusion ticket needed a boost to carry majorities in both houses of the legislature. The legislature would
fill both Senate seats in 1901; the two parties accordingly

poured their utmost into campaigns of obscure candidates for legislative seats.

Like much of the campaign, election day brought a sense of déjà vu. Bryan garnered nearly 6.4 million votes, for 45.5 percent of the total; in 1896 he had taken almost 6.5 million votes and 46.7 percent. McKinley won in 1900 with 7.2 million votes and 51.7 percent; in 1896, he got 7.1 million and 51.1 percent. Bryan took 155 electoral votes in 1900, 176 in 1896. He carried 17 states in 1900, 22 in 1896. While Kentucky returned to the Democratic column in 1900, Bryan lost Washington, giving McKinley a clean sweep of the Pacific coast states. McKinley carried Utah and Wyoming among the Rocky Mountain states, which had been solidly for silver in 1896, and he won the entire Middle West, including Nebraska. Bryan's Fusion allies in Nebraska lost all state-wide offices and the legislature (and, therefore, both seats in the United States Senate).

McKinley swept to victory on the same two campaign themes he had played so persistently in 1896: prosperity and patriotism. In 1896, Bryan had to carry the Democratic standard in a year when the incumbent Democratic president bore the onus of four years of depression; in 1900, Bryan faced an incumbent president able to point to four years of increased employment, higher farm prices, and a fifty percent increase in exports. Silver had lost much of its political potency; imperialism failed to replenish the lost enthusiasm. Even so, silver helped Bryan to carry the mining states of Idaho, Nevada, Montana, and Colorado. Farm prices rose steadily from 1896 to 1900, increasing more rapidly than the consumer price index in most years. As the farmers' financial situation improved, those who had survived the terrible times of the 1890s took less interest in political solutions. Several prominent Populists returned to the GOP, a few others backed the Middle-of-the-Road ticket. Middle-of-the-Road candidates did poorly, drawing only a quarter as many votes as the Prohibition party. Populism had burned itself out as an independent political force. Some foreign-stock voters—especially Germans—disliked imperialism, but that issue sometimes failed to supercede their economic conservatism and suspicion of inflation. Bryan's supporters again pointed to coercion of voters in industrial areas and added charges of fraud, but evidence that coercion and fraud determined the outcome is even less persuasive than for 1896.

Election day 1900 must have seemed to Bryan the end of one career and the beginning of another. Over the previous fifty years, only once had a major party given a second presidential nomination to a candidate who had already lost. *Never* had a party given a losing candidate a third chance. The Republican sweep in Nebraska guaranteed that both Nebraska senators would be from the GOP until 1905 at the earliest. Bryan's future seemed to lie elsewhere than in the field of elective office. Fortunately he had other fields to till. He and Mary had bought a farm on the outskirts of Lincoln and now planned to build a new home on it. He drew throngs when he traveled the national lecture circuit. The books he and Mary wrote continued to sell well; *The Second Battle* appeared on booksellers' shelves before the end of the campaign. Within ten weeks of election day, he launched another project: the first issue of his own newspaper stood ready for press with 17,000 paid subscriptions. The name Bryan chose for the masthead was one a reporter had hung on the young presidential candidate who carried his own suitcase in 1896—*The Commoner*.

V

Between Crusades

FORTY YEARS OLD IN 1900, William Jennings Bryan seemed "prematurely aged" to a reporter who had not seen him since his presidential campaign. His hair line had receded and he had regained the weight he lost in 1898. Lines had appeared about his eyes and mouth. The reporter thought his voice had acquired "a metallic sound, faint but yet distinct." His health remained sound. The reporter noted that the Bryans' farm at the southeast edge of Lincoln gave W.J. room to exercise his favorite saddle horse, Governor, or to practice his carpentry skills by building a chicken house.

The farm also gave Bryan the opportunity to live the life of a country gentleman, much as his father had lived near Salem. Just as Silas had commissioned a brick country home, so now W.J. and Mary planned a large brick home on a rise; the distinctive Queen Anne styling and dramatic corner tower of the new house loomed over the valley of Antelope Creek. W.J. chose the name "Fairview" for their new home, and saw it as a new Monticello with himself as the sage in residence. Though he lived on a farm, he explained to his friends that he was not a farmer but an agriculturist. "An agriculturist lives in the country, earns his living in the city, and spends it on the farm," he explained, but "the farmer lives on the farm, earns his living on it and spends what he earns in the city."

Silas Bryan had built his country home with income de-

William Jennings Bryan with his ever present palm fan and hand-kerchief, as he appeared to thousands of Chautauqua listeners during the early twentieth century; about 1905. (Photograph courtesy of the Nebraska State Historical Society.)

rived from the law and the bench; W.J. and Mary built theirs with income from publishing royalties and lecture fees. Every summer Bryan took to the lecture circuit, usually through the Chautauqua. The name Chautauqua derived from a lake in upstate New York, site of a Methodist Sunday School teacher training program. The blend of inspirational oratory, education, and entertainment that developed there soon spread across the nation, as towns—especially in the Middle West—sponsored week-long programs. "Chautauqua Week" brought hundreds, sometimes thousands of people to town. Many lived on the grounds, sleeping in tents and eating in large dining pavilions. Speakers usually held forth in circus-size tents during early years. Some towns eventually acquired large wooden structures, with barn-like roofs to keep off the blazing summer sun or errant rainstorms, but with no walls to inhibit cooling evening breezes. In the early twentieth century, Chautauqua companies began to tour the country, some with their own trains, stopping for a day or so in each town on their route. At their high point, thousands of towns held annual Chautauqua assemblies. Millions of people came to see political figures, comedians, inspirational orators, or opera; to hear glee clubs, lectures on ancient history, or string quartets; to watch magic-lantern slides of the Holy Land or the building of the Panama Canal. Fireworks displays, boating, and games filled the hours before and after formal presentations.

Before the 1920s, Chautauqua programs emphasized speakers over entertainment, and Bryan delivered more Chautauqua lectures than any other prominent political figure. Nearly every summer for a quarter-century, he spent three months traveling the circuit, delivering 200–300 speeches each year in nearly that many small towns. He usually spoke twice a day on social, religious, educational, and political questions. "He loved the freedom of lecture circuits," Grace later recalled, "the ever changing scenes, and the crowds, for he loved people. Meeting them in all the little towns and hamlets as well as in the great cities, he could better understand their needs; he could better mirror the spirit of democracy which he so ardently expressed." Mary provided a similar view: "When he returned from his tours he had not only spoken to, but had listened to, the mind of America. He had had an opportunity to know what America was thinking and he had helped America to make up her mind."

During the nineteenth century, the central position of speech-making in politics and religion produced great orators. Bryan's star rose toward the end of that tradition; unquestionably he ranks among the very best. Through his lecture tours, his voice put bread on his family's table and kept a roof over their heads. He insisted that admission charges be kept low—he preferred 25 cents a person and did not permit more than 50 cents—but he still did well financially. Few speakers could match the drawing power of his name or the carrying power of his voice. He recalled with amusement the farmer who told him, "You are the only man I ever heard speak that I could see his back teeth all the time he was speaking." Bryan could speak to thirty thousand people in the open air, without amplification, and those on the fringes of the crowd could follow every thought. One evening, Mary stayed in their hotel room to read, with the window open. She heard every word of that night's lecture, even though it was three blocks distant. "His words flowed along like the steady current of a stream," she recalled, and described his voice as having "a reverberating quality."

Speaking was hard work. On a Middle Western summer day, the temperature might hover around 100° outside, and rise even higher inside. Bryan's usual practice was to speak with one hand resting on a block of ice, then to wipe his brow with that hand. The other hand held a palm fan, which he kept in motion; for many Americans, Bryan's palm fan was as much a part of his normal appearance as his simple alpaca coat and string tie. He threw enormous energies into his speaking. The energy he expended in speaking could only be replenished by eating, Bryan believed, and he acquired a reputation for consuming prodigious quantities of food when on the lecture circuit or the campaign trail.

When Bryan spoke on the Chautauqua circuit, or when he spent a month during the winter on the lyceum lecture circuit (a similar undertaking), he seemed to extemporize. He delivered the same speeches over and over, honing the delivery, sharpening the metaphors, testing new phrases, and discarding those that failed to provoke the desired response. According to Grace, who often accompanied him on his tours, Bryan typically centered his comments around one or more of three involuntary relationships experienced by every individual: to God, to society, and to government.

"Man needs faith in God to strengthen him in his hours of trial," he argued in one speech, "and he needs it to give him courage to do the work of life." And, he added, "a sense of responsibility to God is the most potent influence that acts upon a human life." Morality was, for Bryan, "the outward manifestation" of the relation between the individual and God. People observed moral standards because of "the belief that an all-seeing eye scrutinizes every thought and work and act of the individual," and because obedience to divinely established standards was a necessity for eternal life.

Bryan often spoke on the individual's obligation to others. "No one lives unto himself or dies unto himself. The tie that binds each human being to every other human being is one that cannot be severed." For Bryan, "the essential thing is that each person, man or woman, shall recognize the obligation to contribute in helpfulness." He had no use for the "drone," and he looked forward to a day when "each person is entitled to draw from society in proportion as he contributes to the welfare of society." Indeed, in one address, Bryan claimed that "I can not conceive of any way of earning money except to give to society a service equivalent in value to the money collected."

When discussing government, Bryan often cited Thomas Jefferson as his inspiration. In one well-known Chautauqua address, "The Value of an Ideal," Bryan claimed that "the fundamental principle of government" in the United States is that "the people have a right to have what they want in legislation." In other talks, however, he pointed to the duty of government "to restrain those who would interfere with the inalienable rights of the individual." Bryan drew upon Jefferson in defining "inalienable rights," citing "the right to life, the right to liberty, the right to the pursuit of happiness," but he added to Jefferson's list "the right to worship God according to the dictates of one's conscience." He pointed to freedom of speech as "essential to representative government."

Each citizen, Bryan thought, had a clear duty. Beginning with the proposition that "each individual finds his greatest security in the intelligence and happiness of his fellows," and that "the welfare of each [is] the concern of all," Bryan concluded that each citizen "should therefore exert himself to the utmost to improve conditions for all and to raise the level upon which all stand." This obligation tied together Bryan's basic concepts of God, service to others, and government: "He renders the largest service to others when he brings himself into harmony with the law of God, who has made service the measure of greatness."

Bryan spent three to four months each year presenting such homilies in towns and villages across the nation, and often spoke in a similar vein to gatherings of Democrats. He expounded the same verities weekly in his newspaper *The Commoner*. The first issue of the paper ran to eight pages, but that size soon doubled. Its columns featured Bryan's latest speeches, as well as his views on political questions. Household hints and recipes shared space with summaries of world news and advertising for patent medicines. He refused to accept advertising from trusts or monopolies. For the first seven years of the paper's operation, Bryan also published an annual volume of excerpts, *The Commoner Condensed,* mostly speeches and comments on current events.

Operation of the paper required a sizable staff, especially because W.J. left Lincoln for months at a time on the lecture circuit and Mary often accompanied him. Charles W. Bryan, who had come to work for his older brother during the 1896 campaign, took much of the responsibility for managing the newspaper and for overseeing the day-to-day functioning of the Bryan political organization in Nebraska. He shared the latter task with Thomas S. Allen, a Lincoln lawyer who married the Bryan brothers' youngest sister, Mary Elizabeth. Richard Metcalfe, who had produced campaign biographies of W.J. in 1896 and 1900, left the *Omaha World-Herald* to become associate editor of *The Commoner.* "Met," Charles, and Mary all joined W.J. in the operation of the paper, while other staff and writers produced particular departments. One historian who studied the paper concluded that even the careful reader often found it impossible to determine whether a given editorial came from the pen of W.J., Charles, Mary, or Met; their views on issues and their writing styles seemed interchangeable.

While Bryan continued to speak at Jefferson Day banquets and Labor Day parades across the nation, and while he addressed political concerns in the columns of *The Commoner,* he indicated no desire to seek office. He nonetheless remained a prominent political figure. After his defeat in 1900, few seriously considered him a prospect for another presidential nomination. Some expected him to fade gracefully from political view. He did not do so. He took a leading part in the 1902 state convention of the Fusion parties in Nebraska. The Democratic convention had wanted to nominate him for governor, but he refused. Fusion candidates did poorly in Nebraska in 1902, and Democrats fared no better in most other parts of the country.

Bryan and one or more of his family had traveled the United States since 1891 on various speaking engagements;

they soon began to seek wider horizons. They toured Mexico in 1897. In the spring of 1902, Bryan attended the inauguration of the first president of the new Cuban republic. In his comments, he harkened back to the political oratory of 1900 when he observed that the lowering of the American flag and the raising of that of Cuba brought no humiliation to the United States. After a return to Lincoln via Mexico, he began to prepare for another trip. In mid-November 1903, after the annual election campaigns, he and his fifteen-year-old son, William, left for a nine-week tour of the British Isles, western Europe, and Russia. Bryan met some of the most prominent figures of the day, including British Prime Minister Arthur Balfour, Pope Pius X (whom Bryan thought "full of brotherly love"), and Czar Nicholas II, whom Bryan lectured on freedom of speech. For Bryan, the high point of the trip came during the day spent with Count Leo Tolstoy. Bryan described him as "the intellectual giant of Russia, the moral Titan of Europe, and the world's most conspicuous exponent of the doctrine of love." They discussed Tolstoy's belief in nonviolence, an attitude that Bryan came increasingly to study and share.

When W.J. and young William returned from Europe, the 1904 presidential campaign had begun. Nationwide, the Republican party now looked for leadership to Theodore Roosevelt, who had become president in September 1901 when an assassin's bullet felled McKinley. In March 1902, Roosevelt had directed his attorney general to file suit against the Northern Securities Company, a newly formed company uniting three of the nation's largest railroads, and including some of the most powerful figures in the nation's economy, among them J.P. Morgan. The government suit claimed that the formation of the company violated the Sherman Anti-Trust Act. Shortly before the 1902 elections, Roosevelt followed this action with a speaking tour. He focused on the dangers of trusts and promised regulatory action. In the fall, he intervened in a coal miners' strike and persuaded the mining companies to accept a compromise. All this attention directed to restraining corporations and favoring labor allowed Roosevelt to usurp some of Bryan's thunder. The Rough Rider seemed virtually guaranteed of the election to the presidency in his own right in 1904.

While Bryan gave no indication of interest in running against Roosevelt, he refused to endorse any other candidate, preferring instead to speak to principles. William Randolph Hearst soon emerged as the leading presidential contender from Bryan's wing of the party. Hearst, a New York newspaper publisher, had proven a pillar of strength to Bryan in 1896 and 1900. Instead of endorsing Hearst or anyone else, Bryan insisted that the Democrats who had backed him in the past could chose from a multitude of possible candidates. In 1904, Bryan recycled his strategy of 1896, emphasizing principles but playing down commitments to candidates. Perhaps he hoped that presidential lightning would strike a third time. Regardless of such possibilities, his course allowed him to walk into the convention hall as chairman of the Nebraska delegation, with no pledges except to principle.

Held in St. Louis, the convention of 1904 opened with a majority firmly committed to the "reorganizers," those who hoped to return the party to the policies of Cleveland. One of them defined the first task of the convention: "to kill Bryanism, root and branch." The conservative majority preferred Alton B. Parker, a New York judge, as their candidate for president. Bryan faced an uphill struggle. Poor health threatened to restrict his efforts; in the middle of the convention, a physician diagnosed pneumonia in one lung. He would not surrender. He fought for the seating of delegates challenging some reorganizers. He fought in the platform committee to keep his party committed to principles he had upheld in 1896 and 1900. He lost the battle for delegates, but he won the platform. Facing a Resolutions Committee filled with hostile Parker supporters, Bryan initially employed persuasion and logic, but soon he hurled insults as hot as the fever blazing in his temples. He kept in reserve a threat to bolt the party if it denied his principles; he charged that those who opposed him owed allegiance to corporate monopolies. In the end, more of the platform came from Bryan's pen in 1904 than in 1896. It condemned imperialism, high protective tariffs, and trusts and monopolies; it demanded independence for the Philippines and direct election of United States senators. Of Bryan's major issues, only silver and the income tax had disappeared, and neither stood contradicted anywhere in the platform.

Bryan spent all night in the battle over the platform. The next day saw the nomination of presidential candidates, and Bryan planned to speak last. Speeches droned on and on; his chance came after four o'clock in the morning. "Two nights without sleep and a cold make it difficult for me to make myself heard," he began, but his voice and stamina rallied when he began to rip into his subject. He took the podium to second the nomination of a peripheral candidate. In fact, he spoke for himself: "Eight years ago a Democratic national convention placed in my hand the standard of the party . . . Four years later that commission was renewed. I come tonight to this Democratic national convention to return the commission. You may dispute whether I have fought a good fight, you may dispute whether I have finished my course, but you cannot deny that I have kept the faith."

Bryan argued that the election of a Democrat was even more important in 1904 than in 1900. For proof, he pointed to militarism as the animating feature of the Republican convention. But, he asked, "must we choose between a god of war and a god of gold?" After favorable references to Hearst and several other candidates, but not Parker, Bryan seconded the nomination of his choice, then asserted in conclusion that the fundamental issue was "between democracy and plutocracy."

As soon as he finished, Bryan's friends helped him to his hotel room and called medical assistance. While he lay there ill and exhausted, Parker won the nomination on the first ballot. As the convention prepared to take up the nomination of a vice-presidential candidate, the hall began to buzz with the rumor that Parker had indicated that he would not accept the nomination unless the convention endorsed his commitment to the gold standard. Despite his pneumonia, Bryan left his hotel room, returned to the convention floor, and once more flayed the reorganizers. When the convention voted by four to one to send a conciliatory telegram to Parker, Bryan left in defeat and returned to his sickbed.

Bryan went home after the convention, announced he would support Parker, then retreated to Fairview to recuperate. After a rest, he emerged to reaffirm his support for Parker and simultaneously to advocate a set of proposals that must have caused Parker to blanch—government ownership of railroads, the income tax, and election of federal judges. After the Nebraska Fusion conventions, Bryan gave a political speech in Missouri, then retired to Arizona for a month of rest. After this, he filled several Chautauqua commitments. When he finally undertook speaking on Parker's behalf, election day was only a month away. Most of his political efforts ignored Parker and concentrated instead on what he saw as the dangers Roosevelt's election posed; he focused especially on Roosevelt's penchant for militarism and his ties to business.

Despite Bryan's efforts, Roosevelt won the greatest presidential victory in a third of a century, taking 56.2 percent of the vote to Parker's 37.6 percent. Parker carried only the "solid South" as Roosevelt swept the rest of the nation. Tom Watson, running as a Populist, placed a distant fifth; of Watson's votes, nearly one in five came from Nebraska, a striking indication of the extent to which Fusion had kept alive a Populist party in Bryan's state when other state Populist organizations disintegrated. Roosevelt swept Nebraska as he did the rest of the Middle West, sealing off any possibility of Bryan's election to the United States Senate. Bryan began immediately to plan for 1908, hoping to make public owner-ship of municipal utilities and government ownership of rail-roads the issue that might finally take him, or someone who shared his views, into the White House.

Bryan may have begun to plan for 1908 while surveying the wreckage of the Parker campaign, but he also turned his thoughts to travel. Mary had been unable to accompany W.J. and young William on their European tour in 1903. The death of Mary's father in the spring of 1905 freed her to travel and also suggested the need for a diversion from her sorrow. W.J. organized a world tour for the entire family. Except for Ruth, who had recently married and was preg-nant, the Bryan family left San Francisco in the fall of 1905. After a brief stop in Hawaii, the four arrived in Japan. W.J. met the emperor and other leading decision-makers, and was impressed with the economic and social development he witnessed. From Japan, the Bryans traveled to Korea, China, and the Philippines.

Bryan was unprepared for the affectionate welcome he received in the Philippines. "The Filipinos," Grace later re-called, "greeted him as their champion and true friend." As the party traveled throughout the archipelago, crowds met them with banners linking admiration for Bryan to hopes for independence. One cited "W. J. Bryan, Defender of Our Liberty"; another saluted "Mr. Bryan, the Hope of Our Na-tionality." Filipinos who hoped Bryan would speak strongly in favor of independence came away disappointed. He mod-erated his arguments, believing that the proper place for the strongest arguments was in the United States, where the decision had to be made. Traveling throughout the islands brought Bryan strong reinforcement for his commitment to Philippine independence. He discovered no support for American sovereignty among the Filipinos, and he found the Filipinos to be fully capable of self-government. For those hoping to expand American commerce, he suggested that "friends are better customers than enemies."

From the Philippines, the Bryans traveled to Singapore, then to Java, Ceylon, Burma, and India. They crossed the subcontinent by rail from Calcutta to Bombay. Bryan met with Indian leaders, and he concluded that English colonial administration was "far worse, far more burdensome to the people, and far more unjust" than he had expected. He found the British administrators he met to be "the highest type of their countrymen," yet "England acquired India for England's advantage, not for India's," and the rest followed inevitably. From Bombay, the Bryans crossed by ship to Egypt, where the visage of a 4,000-year-old wooden statue reminded him of Mark Hanna. From Egypt, the party went to Beirut and Damascus, then to the Holy Land, Greece, and Turkey. After seeing Constantinople, they bade farewell to Asia, Bryan noting that while "we have enjoyed the experiences," they had not "fallen in love with Asiatic food."

From Turkey, the party journeyed first to Bulgaria, then on to the Austro-Hungarian Empire, where they visited Budapest, Prague, and Vienna. A trip through Russia brought them to St. Petersburg, where Bryan found hope for the emergence of "a free, self-governing and prosperous nation." In Sweden, he applauded King Oscar II for having superintended the separation of that nation from Norway without recourse to war, then the party traveled to Norway to witness the coronation of the king. Democrat to the core, Bryan nevertheless acknowledged that the Norwegian people had selected their form of government and their king; this seemed to him in keeping with his principle that "people have a right to have whatever form of government they desire." After the family donned their most formal attire and moved through a receiving line, Bryan concluded, "the more an American sees of [royal pomp and pageantry], the more he appreciates the simplicity of public life in his own country."

In Great Britain, Bryan was granted an audience with the king, and Bryan found reassuring "his personal interest in the promotion of peace." He also met with members of the new Liberal government. The triumph of the Liberals, he believed, marked "a victory for progressive, democratic ideas." At a July Fourth reception given by the American ambassador, Bryan met both Winston Churchill—he thought him "a brilliant young man"—and J. P. Morgan, also a visitor to London. While there, he spoke on the subject of peace at the meeting of the Interparliamentary Union. "If we are to build permanent peace," he declared, "it must be on the foundation of the brotherhood of man." From Britain, the party traveled to Holland, Germany, Switzerland, Italy, France, and Spain, and finally back to the United States.

When the Bryans' ship arrived in New York in late August 1906, a host of prominent Democrats, including many Nebraskans, swarmed to meet them. Jim Dahlman, now mayor of Omaha, came with lariat in hand and lassoed Bryan. The Commercial Travelers Anti-Trust League sponsored a reception in Madison Square Garden, where an audience of 12,000 awaited the speech Bryan had crafted during the ocean journey. Their repeated cheers before he began to speak brought tears to his eyes. He came, he said, with a message of peace from the Interparliamentary Union meeting, where he found encouraging signs for the growth of arbitration as an alternative to war. He assured the crowd "that our nation has lost prestige rather than gained it by our experiment with colonialism." Bryan reported with pleasure that the income tax, "which some in our country have denounced as a socialistic attack upon wealth," had "the indorsement of the most conservative countries in the old world." He called for settling labor disputes peacefully through the establishment of "a permanent, impartial board"; he also opposed the use of injunctions in labor disputes, and advocated the eight-hour work day.

Bryan then buried the silver issue. "The unlooked-for and

William Jennings Bryan exhorting the faithful in Madison Square Garden, 1906, upon returning from his family's trip around the world. (Photograph courtesy of the Nebraska State Historical Society.)

unprecedented increase in the production of gold has brought a victory to both the advocates of gold and the advocates of bimetallism—the former keeping the gold standard which they wanted and the latter securing the larger volume of money for which they contended." He declared himself satisfied with the partial victory and invited the "friends of monometallism" to join now "in the effort to restore to the people the rights which have been gradually taken from them by the trusts." After a survey of the problems posed by great corporate power, he predicted that in 1908 "the paramount issue" would be "the trust issue." He denied that the Republicans could provide effective remedy for the problem, because they had "built up through special legislation the very abuses which need to be eradicated." Equating trusts with monopolies, he then turned to remedies. Persuaded that only part of the solution could come from enforcement of the Sherman Anti-Trust Act, he argued that additional legislation would be also necessary. A federal license law would provide a basis for regulation, and he proposed denying tariff protection to items produced by monopolies, a remedy he had first suggested when in Congress.

New railroad regulations had recently become law, but Bryan raised the possibility that the increased powers recently bestowed upon the Interstate Commerce Commission (ICC) would encourage railroad companies to seek greater influence over the president, who appointed ICC members. Railroads formed a special aspect of the trust issue; Bryan presented his solution to the railroad question: "Railroads partake so much of the nature of a monopoly that they must ultimately become public property and be managed by public officials in the interest of the whole community." He proposed that only the trunk lines be federally owned and operated, and the local lines reserved to state governments. The major European nations, he noted, all provided examples of the effectiveness of government ownership.

Denying that his proposals partook of socialism, Bryan

presented them instead as a means of combatting socialism. "The best way to oppose socialism is to remedy the abuses which have grown up under individualism but which are not a necessary part of individualism." He closed his speech with an indictment of plutocracy, accusing it of defiling and polluting business, despoiling the home, disgracing religion, and oppressing the people. To many of Bryan's followers, his Madison Square Garden speech sounded the call for yet another presidential bid and dispelled any notion that he might try to run to the right of the Roosevelt administration.

V I

Progressive Crusades

BY THE TIME the Bryan family returned to the United States from their world tour, the 1906 campaign had begun. The Fusion parties in Nebraska held their conventions before Bryan returned, although the Populist party mustered but a feeble remnant of its past numbers. The Nebraska Republicans that year followed the reformist path marked out by Theodore Roosevelt when they nominated candidates who pledged to remove railroad influences from government. Bryan made his usual speeches, but his state voted solidly Republican.

Bryan also spent a good deal of time campaigning in Oklahoma, a territory then electing delegates to a constitutional convention as a prelude to statehood. He took heart from the overwhelming Democratic victory there. Invited to address the convention, he instead sent a long, thoughtful letter outlining a series of proposals; nearly all were adopted. The draft constitution included the direct primary, the initiative and referendum, provisions to expedite public ownership, controls on corporations, protections for labor, and election of nearly all governmental decision-makers. Ratification of the document prompted a major struggle, with most Republicans opposing and most Democrats in support. Secretary of War William Howard Taft, already emerging as Roosevelt's chosen successor, was the best known of many Republicans to speak against ratification; Bryan spoke extensively in defense of the proposed constitution. Ratification carried by more than 70 percent, and Democratic candidates for state office won equally impressive victories. When Bryan accepted an invitation to address the new legislature, the chaplain opened the session by invoking divine intercession on Bryan's behalf in the 1908 campaign. As one of its first acts, the new state government adopted a bank deposit insurance measure similar to that Bryan advocated as the solution to the wave of bank failures accompanying the Panic of 1907.

Bryan believed that Oklahomans had achieved not only the

William Jennings Bryan accepting his third Democratic nomination for the presidency, on the steps of the Nebraska Capitol, 1908. (Photograph courtesy of the Nebraska State Historical Society.)

best constitution of any state, but also "a better constitution than the constitution of the U.S." He covered its innovations in detail in the columns of *The Commoner,* and he incorporated many features into his plans for the 1908 Democratic platform. The drive for a third nomination, begun with the Madison Square Garden speech in 1906, gathered momentum through the next two years. By February 1908, his brother Charles had sent out more than 120,000 letters urging supporters to take the lead in their neighborhoods and to form clubs designed to guarantee "that platforms and candidates were selected that represented the will of the rank and file of the party," something the Bryan brothers considered synonymous with choosing delegates pledged to Bryan. When the Democratic convention opened in Denver, Bryan held the two-thirds majority necessary for nomination. Only the final wording of the platform remained. As in 1900, Bryan followed tradition and did not attend the convention. Charles served as W.J.'s spokesman on platform issues, the two conferring frequently via a special telegraph line installed between Denver and Fairview.

The platform contained nearly every proposal Bryan had promoted over the previous half-dozen years. Proclaiming the need "to free the Government from the grip of those who have made it a business asset of the favor-seeking corporations," the platform declared "the overshadowing issue" to be: "Shall the people rule?" The platform stood silent, however, on government ownership of railroads and on the initiative and referendum, both concessions intended to promote party unity. It called for regulation of corporations, tariff reform, an insurance fund to protect bank depositors, an income tax, the direct election of senators, and independence for the Philippines. The Democrats courted the American Federation of Labor (AFL) by advocating the eight-hour day for government workers, a cabinet-level Department of Labor, recognition of the right of workers to organize, and changes in the laws relating to injunctions.

Labor leaders had asked the Republican convention for similar pledges, but they left empty-handed. Samuel Gompers, president of the AFL, came to Denver to confer personally on the platform; he left pleased and fully supportive of Bryan's candidacy. For the vice-presidency, the convention nominated John Kern of Indiana.

Nearly a month before the Democrats shouted their support for Bryan and his platform, the Republican convention had nominated Roosevelt's choice, William Howard Taft. Though he had little previous experience as a candidate for elective office, Taft had served in a series of appointive positions as judge, governor of the Philippines, and Secretary of War. The two presidential candidates shared reputations as genial men of hearty appetite. Taft stood slightly taller than Bryan, but outweighed him by nearly a hundred pounds. Both had wed strong-willed women who took active roles in promoting their husbands' careers. Taft lacked Bryan's enthusiasm for public speaking; he undertook the task only to head off Bryan, whom he considered an irresponsible rabble-rouser "in favor of the punishment of the rich, but opposed to a strong government."

In 1896 and 1900, Bryan had launched his campaign with acceptance speeches in New York and Indiana, states he deemed vital to success. In 1908, he accepted the nomination in Lincoln, on the steps of the state capitol. In his speech, he defined the paramount question of 1908: "Shall the people rule?" All other issues, he proclaimed, formed only separate manifestations of this single question. "Shall the people control their own Government and use that Government for the protection of their rights and for the promotion of their welfare?" he asked, "Or shall the representatives of predatory wealth prey upon a defenseless public, while the offenders secure immunity from subservient officials whom they raise to power by unscrupulous methods?"

Bryan noted that Roosevelt and Taft both pointed to abuses by corporate power; he then indicted Republicans for their conduct of government during the time when those abuses appeared. "For a generation," he maintained, "the Republican party has drawn its campaign funds from the beneficiaries of special legislation." He declared that party unable to "attack wrongdoing in high places without disgracing many of its prominent members"; as a result, the party of Roosevelt and Taft used "opiates instead of the surgeon's knife." The Nebraskan called upon Taft to follow his own example by refusing corporate contributions, limiting individual contributions to $10,000, and identifying all contributors of more than $100. Again and again he asked, "Shall the people rule?" He always found Democratic success essential for an affirmative response. Bryan closed with a promise: if elected, he would create "a government in which the people rule."

Bryan briefly hoped for a less hectic campaign pace than before, but he soon found himself on the circuit, delivering several speeches a day—his record in 1908 was twenty-four in one day—and sleeping in lurching railroad cars. "Shall the people rule?" formed the constant watchword as he tied issue after issue to the tail of that kite. The platform promise for a federal bank deposit insurance program appeared in many speeches. In urban areas, he stressed the labor planks. Corruption of the political process by corporations formed a third prominent theme.

In 1896, Bryan had seemed a voice in the wilderness when he spoke against the power of corporations; by 1908, he was one of a multitude. Between 1905 and 1908, scores of governors had joined in the outcry against corporate influence in government, nineteen of them in 1907 alone. During the years 1904 to 1906, a wave of journalistic exposures of governmental corruption had prompted states to approve laws limiting the power of corporations in politics, regulating railroads (usually by state commissions), and establishing the direct primary. For the moment, at least, the tenets of anti-monopolism had moved from groups on the fringes of po-

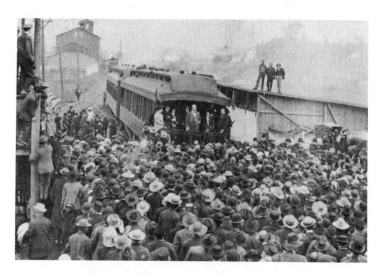

William Jennings Bryan campaigning from the rear platform of a train, in Kentucky; probably 1908. (Photograph courtesy of the Nebraska State Historical Society.)

litical activity—such as the Populists—to the center ring of American politics.

Bryan's calls for the limitation of corporate power found many echoes now; so did his insistence that people had obligations to their fellows, especially those less fortunate. His lectures on the Chautauqua circuit since 1900 had often emphasized the ideal of service to others, something Bryan considered "applied Christianity." As early as 1903, he suggested that Christ's injunction to "love thy neighbor as thyself" held the potential to "solve every problem economic, social, political, and religious." Bryan's social views put him close to a group of reformers whose reading of the Scriptures led them to propose social reforms, a group often identified as advocates of a "Social Gospel."

In both his anti-monopolism and his commitment to the

Social Gospel, Bryan spoke some of the language of what, in 1910 and 1911, came to be called "progressivism." Taft, and Taft's champion, Roosevelt, shared some of the phrases of progressivism with Bryan, most notably those denoting opposition to corporate influences in government. Roosevelt had launched anti-trust forays against a few large corporations, and had endorsed legislation regulating railroads and meatpacking. Roosevelt described himself as a "radical on the conservative side"; he thought Taft to be the same. Taft fully supported Roosevelt's accomplishments; he announced in 1907 that "Mr. Roosevelt's views were mine long before I knew Mr. Roosevelt at all." Roosevelt believed popular support for his administration's policies meant that Taft would be elected *"if we can keep things as they are."* He proved an accurate prophet.

Bryan mounted his usual strenuous campaign, concentrating on the Middle West and New York, just as he had done in 1896 and 1900. He still drew enormous crowds. Thousands still responded to his pleas to contribute as little as thirty cents to his campaign. Half of his funds came in amounts of less than $100; only eight contributions exceeded $1,000. In all, Democratic fund raising netted almost $630,000, far less than the $1,656,000 the Republicans realized. The AFL mounted the most vigorous campaign it had ever undertaken for a presidential candidate. Several prominent black leaders gave Bryan their support; the nation's largest German-language newspaper also endorsed him. Despite Taft's Unitarianism, some Catholic voters seemed to lean toward him because of his accomplishments as governor of the Philippines. A few employers issued threats similar to those of 1896 and 1900, making continued employment contingent upon a Taft victory.

When the votes were counted, Bryan lost for the third time. He garnered slightly more votes than in 1900, but fewer than in 1896; his 43.1 percent of the popular vote marked a drop of a few points below his previous share.

Taft drew 51.6 percent, almost exactly the same as McKinley in 1900. Bryan won 162 electoral votes to 321 for Taft, an improvement for Bryan over 1900, but fewer than he had taken in 1896. Bryan carried the "solid South," but beyond the states that had formed the Confederacy he won only five: Kentucky and Oklahoma (the latter voting for president for the first time), the silver states of Colorado and Nevada, and Nebraska. A very close vote in Maryland resulted in Bryan's securing several electoral votes, although Taft got more popular votes there. Two-thirds of the eligible voters took part, down from almost four-fifths in 1896. Even with this decline in turnout, the rate of voter participation for this last Bryan presidential bid has never been matched since then.

Bryan's final presidential campaign failed to touch off the enthusiasm his previous campaigns aroused. Some blamed the failure on the lack of a "paramount" issue, arguing that "Shall the People Rule?" held neither the appeal of free silver in 1896 nor that of anti-imperialism in 1900. One reporter who accompanied Bryan in 1908 thought Bryan spent the entire campaign testing "issue after issue, trying to find a good paramounter," only to dismiss them as "duds." The one issue probably central in most voters' minds could never work to Bryan's favor. Friend and foe alike saw the election as a referendum on the previous seven years of Theodore Roosevelt. When Bryan accused Taft of being a front for Roosevelt, he only said what most voters believed. They knew that Roosevelt had hand-picked his successor; the election results suggest that a majority of voters not only approved of the Roosevelt administration but wanted more of the same. Voters had demonstrated repeatedly since 1896 that a majority considered themselves Republicans; nothing in 1908 gave them reason to change their minds. With his strong personal following, Bryan probably ran better than any other candidate the Democrats might have named; thus he saved Statehouses, Congressional seats, and local offices for his party in some close contests. In the House of Representatives, the Republicans showed a net loss of three, while the Democrats gained eight. Bryan must have been especially pleased by results in Nebraska, where Democrats won the governorship, half of the Congressional seats, and majorities in the state legislature.

Bryan seems never to have understood the reasons for his defeat in 1908. In 1896 and 1900, he could blame it on coercion and corruption, but in 1908 he opened the columns of *The Commoner* to readers' analyses. When many of the responses pointed to defections by Catholics, Bryan felt deeply puzzled because he had fought valiantly against anti-Catholic bigotry from the beginning of his political career. He saw no reason for Catholics to desert him. A few respondents also claimed that the liquor trade had given strong support to Taft, apparently from distrust of Bryan's well-known personal temperance. Nearly a year after the election, Bryan announced his decision never to seek a presidential nomination again, although he said nothing about a draft.

Once the election had passed, Bryan took an interest in events in Lincoln, for the organization he had developed to carry Nebraska had put a Democrat in the governor's office. For the first time since statehood, Nebraska Democrats held majorities in both houses of the legislature. Most of the men who walked the corridors of the state capitol had stood by Bryan since the turbulent struggles for control of the state party in the mid-1890s; they welcomed the opportunity to translate proposals into law. In the governor's office sat Ashton C. Shallenberger, a small-town banker and an ardent silverite from the 1890s. He named Arthur F. Mullen as his chief patronage dispenser and liaison to the legislature. A red-haired lawyer of Irish parentage, Mullen had entered politics in the 1890s as a Populist. Bryan recruited him early in 1908 to build a state organization that would carry Nebraska. Mullen had traveled throughout the state, convincing old-time Populists to become active Democrats and reorganizing moribund county committees.

Shallenberger and Mullen pushed a broad agenda of reform through the legislature during its three-month session in 1909. In fulfillment of both state and national platforms, the Nebraska Democrats passed bank deposit insurance legislation, similar to that of Oklahoma, requiring all state-chartered banks to pay into a deposit insurance fund. Bryan must have been pleased to see his state take the lead in implementing the promises of the platform he had drafted the year before. Bryan found fault with the 1909 legislature, however, for failing to pass an initiative and referendum measure. Mullen blamed the legislature's rejection on lobbying by the liquor industry, which feared that the initiative might be used to restrict its trade. Although most Democratic legislators needed little prompting, the liquor lobby had also urged the legislature to reject "county option," an issue destined to play a major role in state politics.

County option had emerged as a potent political issue in a relatively short time, primarily as a result of activities by the Anti-Saloon League. Proudly describing itself as "the Church in action against the saloon," the League had originated with a meeting in Washington, D.C., in 1895. During the following decade, it became such a well-organized, single-minded force that it captured the support of most temperance advocates and established itself nationally as the leading force opposed to alcohol. Its strength and its organizational base came from churches, especially Methodists, Baptists, Congregationalists, and Presbyterians. Chapters within individual churches provided the core of League activists, many of them women, as well as the bulk of its financial support.

As its name implied, the League focused much of its antagonism against the saloon. By attacking the saloon, the League chose what it considered the least defensible element in the liquor industry. As League publications and activities made clear, they did not just oppose the saloon, but liquor itself. League publications credited alcohol with everything from increasing the divorce rate to causing prostitution, epilepsy, and poverty. During the early twentieth century, the League became the major organizing force in the drive that eventually produced nation-wide prohibition.

The League and other temperance organizations presented arguments in language that evangelical Protestants found highly persuasive. Religious arguments always formed the central element in this rhetoric. The perfectionist impulse present in Methodism and other Protestant bodies led them to the view that the perfection of at least some elements of society through law was possible, as well as desirable. Increasingly, these groups came to see liquor as a force that damaged lives, destroyed families, inhibited conversion, and held significant political power. As churches came to label alcohol the most significant obstacle to a better society, wine even vanished from the Communion table as many Protestant churches replaced it with grape juice. Adherents of the Social Gospel saw prohibition as one of several social reforms needed to improve the lives of those who suffered from the impacts of industrialization and urbanization.

Those who opposed alcohol on religious grounds received support in the early twentieth century from other quarters. Scientific investigation of the physiological effects of alcohol revealed important connections to several diseases and found new information on the narcotic and depressive qualities of the drug. Some scientists began to suggest that any use of alcohol posed a danger to health, and school texts began to echo temperance views that alcohol was a poison. Sociologists added studies showing links from liquor to prostitution, venereal disease, poverty, crime, and broken families. Other evidence pointed to alcohol as contributing to industrial accidents and inefficiency on the job. Reformers condemned it as well for corrupting the political process. Saloons had long been closely identified with political organizations that dominated many large cities, and criticism of political machines, such as New York's Tammany Hall, often came to include saloons as part of the problem. Demonstrations of the political appeal of prohibition began to appear. Alabama, Georgia, and Oklahoma voted themselves dry in 1907, and Mississippi and North Carolina followed in 1908, thereby doubling the number of dry states within the space of only two years.

Bryan had always been a teetotaler. Throughout his years in Nebraska politics, however, he had lived with the knowledge that his party drew its greatest strength in Nebraska from the opponents of prohibition, from Germans, Czechs, Irish, and Poles who disagreed that drinking was sinful. After nearly twenty years of silence on liquor, he now began to pick up the prohibitionist arguments he had written down in the 1880s, encouraged perhaps by the political success of the Anti-Saloon League and by the Nebraska legislature's efforts to deal with the issue in 1909.

Formed in 1897, the Nebraska Anti-Saloon League developed slowly over the following decade. State law provided that a town or village might vote to prohibit the sale of alcohol within its boundaries; by 1908, 450 towns had voted themselves dry. Temperance advocates found the local option law inadequate, however, for saloonkeepers sometimes moved just outside legal boundaries of dry communities. Many temperance supporters believed that rural voters were more likely to vote for temperance than urbanites because they were not in close proximity to a saloon every day. The League and its allies therefore sought to move the unit of decision-making from town to county as a means of combatting the saloon. In 1908, George Sheldon, the incumbent Republican governor, favored county option. Shallenberger made clear his opposition to county option and won support from the liquor industry. When Shallenberger ran ahead of

Bryan in Nebraska, temperance advocates charged that saloonkeepers had scratched Bryan for Taft.

Shallenberger and Mullen understood both the realities of the Nebraska Democratic party's voter base and the political volatility of the county option movement. They set out to disarm the liquor issue. They proposed not to deny Nebraskans the right to buy liquor, but instead to require saloons to close between 8:00 P.M. and 7:00 A.M. Mullen forced the measure through the legislature, assisted by temperance-minded Republicans; Shallenberger gave great publicity to the intense pressures to veto, which liquor interests placed on him. Then he finally signed and, in Mullen's words, "made Nebraska nights as dry as Death Valley."

Bryan had given little indication of preferring either the Daylight Saloon Bill or county option as this drama unfolded. When liquor industry lobbyists and prohibition advocates descended upon Shallenberger to push their views, neither of the Bryan brothers appeared. Late in 1909, W.J. and Mary seemed preoccupied in planning a gala reception at Fairview to celebrate their twenty-fifth wedding anniversary. Once that event passed, W.J. left on a lecture tour, while Mary and Grace traveled to Arizona; there William, Jr., lived with his recent bride. W.J. soon joined Mary and his daughters—Ruth had just gone through a divorce—and together they toured Cuba, then Central and South America. Before leaving, Bryan guaranteed a stormy homecoming when he announced he would introduce a county option plank at the 1910 Nebraska Democratic convention.

Arthur Mullen later charged that Bryan manipulated the 1910 elections in order to defeat his rivals within the Nebraska Democratic party. Mullen's accusations rest upon presumption rather than evidence, but Bryan's course did have the effect of severely splintering the Democratic party of his state, and of irreparably damaging his own party standing. The liquor issue dominated most aspects of state politics that year. Jim Dahlman, mayor of Omaha, had greeted the Daylight Saloon Law with scorn and made clear that he had no intention of enforcing it. Dahlman had been one of the first and one of the most hard-working of Bryan's supporters. When Dahlman announced that he intended to seek the Democratic nomination for governor against Shallenberger in the 1910 primary, some saw Bryan's hand in the decision. Bryan considered making a try for the U.S. Senate seat in 1910; because he did not want to appear to be an office-seeker, he waited for a draft to develop. Gilbert M. Hitchcock quickly lined up support for his own candidacy and took a solid lead. Bryan abandoned his plans to seek the senatorial nomination.

When Nebraska Republicans met in their state convention, they endorsed county option by an overwhelming vote. The Democratic convention included many of Bryan's closest supporters from the previous two decades, but nearly all of them opposed county option. Hitchcock moved that all proposed platform planks be referred to the platform committee without floor discussion, a move intended to prevent Bryan from speaking on the county option issue before the committee could formulate a position. Bryan opposed Hitchcock's motion, but lost by a vote of 394 to 465, an omen of what was to come. Bryan himself served on the platform committee and brought a minority report endorsing county option to the floor of the convention.

Bryan had not faced so hostile a crowd in a state Democratic convention since 1893. He began by disclaiming responsibility for introducing the liquor issue into the state's politics. "I met an issue after it had been introduced, and if I have any apologies to offer, I shall not offer them to the liquor interests for speaking now; I shall offer them to the fathers and mothers of this state for not speaking sooner." He claimed that he had not made up his mind to fight the issue until he discovered a "conspiracy" of brewery interests and other special interests to dominate the state through the Democratic party. "Which side will you take?" he asked his party. "Will you put the Democratic party on the moral side, or will you put it on the immoral side?" The convention delegates rejected both his logic and his county option plank by the lopsided margin of 647 to 198.

In the Democratic primary election, Dahlman edged out Shallenberger by only 304 votes of nearly 55,000; Hitchcock easily took the senatorial nomination. Both the Republican platform and the Republican gubernatorial candidate, Chester Aldrich, proclaimed strong commitments to county option; Aldrich rapidly became the favorite of the temperance advocates. Dahlman proclaimed that, if elected, he would throw a free beer party on the grounds of the state capitol. For more than twenty years, Bryan had no more committed or active supporter than Dahlman. Their political endeavors had long since led to a close friendship as well. Putting principles above friendship and personal loyalties, Bryan announced that he could not endorse Dahlman. "His position on the liquor question," Bryan said, "makes that impossible." The Commoner did not stand alone in bolting Dahlman. Many others from his wing of the state party, and many old-time Populists, joined in supporting Aldrich. The state Anti-Saloon League ran a strong campaign against Dahlman, and Protestant churches became rallying points for the Aldrich cause.

Late in the campaign, Edgar Howard, a long-time Bryan ally and editor of the *Columbus Telegram*, charged that Hitchcock had benefitted from the misuse of state funds in the 1890s. Once again, some saw the hand of Bryan in an effort to defeat a potentially strong Democratic candidate. Bryan kept his distance from the Howard-Hitchcock dispute, however, and refused to comment upon it in *The Commoner*. Howard's course seems most likely to have been his own attempt to deny Hitchcock a role in the leadership of the state party. Dahlman lost, but Hitchcock won; Democrats also won majorities in the state legislature. Bryan's party now became increasingly factionalized, with groups headed by

Hitchcock, Dahlman, Shallenberger and Mullen, and the Bryan brothers. Shallenberger, Mullen, and Dahlman soon found more in common with Hitchcock than with Bryan, and the three-time presidential candidate found himself more and more isolated in Nebraska politics.

Despite the traumas of Nebraska politics, Bryan took pleasure from the strong showing his party made in the 1910 elections across the nation. Several of his supporters, including his running mate from 1908, John Kern, won election to the Senate. Democrats wrested enough Congressional seats from Republicans to give the House of Representatives a Democratic majority for the first time since the onset of depression in 1893. Champ Clark, of Missouri, a long-time Bryan friend, would wield the gavel as Speaker of the House when Congress convened.

With the Nebraska campaign over, the Bryans resumed their increasingly peripatetic lifestyle. Even in mid-1910, with state politics at a boiling stage, W.J. had gone to New York in May to address the Lake Mohonk Peace Conference, and in June both he and Mary traveled to Edinburgh, Scotland. There W.J. attended the Ecumenical Council as a delegate from the Presbyterian Church. Although the Bryans usually worshipped at the small Methodist church near Fairview, they kept their formal membership in Westminster Presbyterian, Lincoln's most prestigious congregation. The winter of 1910–1911 found the Bryans in Texas, where W.J. had recently purchased a 200-acre farm while on one of his lecture tours. W.J. and Grace both thoroughly enjoyed the new environment. Mary had never liked the harsh Nebraska winters, but she found the aridity of the Rio Grande valley no more pleasing. The spring of 1911 brought W.J. to Washington for the opening of a special session of the new Congress. Bryan made the rounds of his friends and allies who now held positions of power in the House, advocating the measures of the 1908 platform and especially tariff revision. In November 1911, he, Mary, and their grandson,

John (Ruth's son, raised as much by W.J. and Mary as by his mother) left for a cruise of the Caribbean. En route to Jamaica, they were shipwrecked, and suffered anxious hours before they were rescued. Upon his return to the United States, Bryan convinced Congressional Democrats to add additional safeguards for ocean travel.

By then, William Howard Taft had splintered the Republican party even more thoroughly than Bryan had divided the Democrats of Nebraska. Taft considered his principal task the administration of the Roosevelt reforms, not their extension. His handling of the tariff alienated a sizable bloc within his party. When Republican Progressives tried to limit the sweeping powers of the Speaker of the House, Taft backed the Speaker even though he had little respect for the man. Although Taft's administration launched far more anti-trust suits than had Roosevelt's, he found it difficult to convince progressives of his sincerity. Challenged in the 1912 presidential primaries by both Senator Robert La Follette, a progressive from Wisconsin, and former President Theodore Roosevelt, Taft lost most of the primaries. Still, he demonstrated the powers of an incumbent president by winning renomination at the Republican convention. Roosevelt and his supporters took the defeat poorly, and began to discuss a third-party candidacy.

Democrats could scarcely contain their glee at the divisions within Republican ranks. Bryan kept his promise to forego a fourth nomination. A number of Democratic candidates emerged: Champ Clark, Speaker of the House of Representatives; Governors Woodrow Wilson of New Jersey and Judson Harmon of Ohio; Congressman Oscar Underwood of Alabama; and several favorite sons. Dismissing Harmon and Underwood as conservatives, Bryan cautioned his brother Charles that *The Commoner* should do nothing "that discriminates against either Wilson or Clark," and specified that the paper must remain "*absolutely neutral*" between them. Bryan recognized that both had made records as progressives, although Clark's support for Bryanite programs dated to 1892, and Wilson's conversion to the progressive cause had come only in the previous two years. Bryan asked Nebraska Democrats to elect him as a convention delegate, promising to accept the outcome of the state's presidential preference primary as binding. By the time Clark won that primary, Bryan had developed doubts about the Speaker. Despite his doubts, he maintained his public stance of neutrality and renewed his pledge to support the Nebraska primary victor.

The 1912 Democratic Convention met in Baltimore. As his party's most prominent leader for sixteen years, Bryan received as much attention as the announced candidates. Speculation ran rampant that he would try to win a fourth nomination for himself. Conservatives wanted to elect Alton B. Parker as temporary chairman of the convention and keynote speaker. When Bryan announced his opposition to Parker, Clark seemed unwilling to join the fight, a decision that Bryan considered tantamount to selling out to Wall Street. Clark's supporters tried to placate Bryan by offering him the permanent chairmanship but, as usual, he refused to compromise. When Parker's name was placed before the convention as candidate for temporary chairman, Bryan nominated John Kern, his running mate in 1908. Kern asked Parker to withdraw in the interests of harmony; when Parker refused, Kern withdrew and nominated Bryan. Bryan accepted the challenge. One Texas delegate shouted his support for Bryan because, as always, "Bryan is on one side and Wall Street is on the other." Bryan lost by a vote of 579 to 508. Thousands of telegrams, praising those who had supported Bryan and berating those who had not, rained upon the delegates. Strengthened by this support, Bryan used his position on the Resolutions Committee to write most of the party's platform, just as he had written much of it at the previous four conventions. Not surprisingly, the platform mirrored his views on nearly every current issue, save only prohibition.

Bryan thought the time not yet propitious for the cold water reform to appear in the national platform.

Bryan's brother Charles discovered what seemed reliable information that the New York delegation planned to shift from Harmon to Clark early in the balloting. The Bryans considered the New York delegates to be under the control of Wall Street; W.J. therefore assumed that Clark's supporters had cut some deal to make the Speaker the choice of big business. Having defined the convention as a battle between the forces of progressivism and those of Wall Street, Bryan prepared to defeat the money power. He flung down the gauntlet by introducing an audacious resolution:

> *Resolved,* That . . . we hereby declare ourselves opposed to the nomination of any candidate for President who is the representative of or under obligation to J. Pierpont Morgan, Thomas F. Ryan [a prominent financier and delegate from Virginia], August Belmont [another well-known financier and delegate from New York], or any other member of the privilege-hunting and favor-seeking class.
>
> *Be It Further Resolved,* That we demand the withdrawal from this convention of any delegate or delegates constituting or representing the above-named interests.

Pandemonium reigned in the convention hall. Bryan had not expected so great a tumult. He commented that, for the "surgical operation" he proposed, "it was possibly a mistake not to have administered chloroform." Delegates accused him of trying to destroy the party, while others praised him for seeking to save it. He withdrew the second clause of the resolution, but few delegates heard him because of the outcry. Given the phrasing of the resolution, opposition became almost impossible. The Commoner chalked up a victory, by a vote of 883 to $201\frac{1}{2}$. A London newspaper compared the Bryan resolution to St. George slaying the dragon; Bryan modestly claimed only that he had prevented the nomination of anyone supported by Wall Street.

Balloting began the next day, but Bryan feared that his presence might set off a demonstration for him as the candidate. He stayed in his hotel room until the tenth ballot, when New York shifted its votes to Clark and gave the Speaker a majority, although less than the two-thirds necessary. Usually, accomplishment of a majority signaled shifts from other candidates; Clark prepared to send a telegram accepting the nomination. As the roll call proceeded past New York, however, Wilson and Underwood supporters quickly combined efforts to stem any rush to Clark. True to his promise to support the winner of the Nebraska primary, Bryan continued to cast his vote for Clark, thinking that New York would soon move to Underwood and that the votes of progressives could then nominate Clark. In Bryan's mind, support from New York disqualified a candidate; he vowed to do whatever was necessary to prevent the nomination of any person with the New York delegation's backing.

On the fourteenth ballot, with New York still behind Clark, Bryan announced a change in his vote from Clark to Wilson, with the promise that he would abandon Wilson if the New Jersey governor secured the support of the New York delegation. Balloting continued two more days. On the forty-sixth ballot, Wilson finally secured the two-thirds majority to become the nominee. Bryan's dramatic shift carried less weight in the final Wilson victory than did Wilson organizers' ability to win over conservatives such as Underwood. Still, Bryan believed that his anti-Wall Street posturing had succeeded in preventing big business from choosing the Democratic nominee, and he trumpeted that view to the nation.

Roosevelt made good his threat to form a third party, the Progressive Party, and the fall campaign became a three-way contest. Bryan contributed generous amounts of advice to the Wilson campaign headquarters. After completing his summer Chautauqua tour and taking a short rest, he devoted two months to the Wilson cause, speaking wherever

Wilson's organizers asked, and closing with his traditional tour of Nebraska. Roosevelt and Taft split the Republican votes, their combined total nearly equalling that polled by Taft alone in 1908. Wilson garnered 41.9 percent of the vote, a smaller share of the total than Bryan had won in any of his campaigns; Wilson also got fewer popular votes than any of Bryan's totals. Given the Republican disarray, however, Wilson carried forty states and took nearly all the electoral votes.

The Democrats' sixteen years of wandering in the wilderness had finally come to an end. Party loyalists across the nation eagerly anticipated opportunities to enact the platform promises of the past five campaigns and to reap the bounty of federal patronage. Because Bryan had spent so much time traveling the nation for so many years, he undoubtedly knew far more Democratic party members than any other person. William G. McAdoo, Wilson's secretary of the treasury, thought Bryan "had a personal acquaintance with more people . . . than any other man in the United States." Nearly all Bryan's acquaintances, it seemed, asked his help in securing jobs with the new administration. Wilson proved receptive to Bryan's advice on a host of matters, but he and his closest political confidant, Colonel Edward House, thought Bryan a poor judge of men. Nonetheless, Wilson met with Bryan in mid-December to elicit his views on a range of appointments and to offer the Commoner the most important position of all, that of secretary of state. When Wilson held out the offer, Bryan asked if Wilson would allow him to seek conciliation treaties. Wilson gave an affirmative response, and the Commoner then asked if he would object should he and Mary refuse to serve alcohol at state functions. The President-elect thought that decision up to them. Bryan accepted. Next to the presidency itself, the position would present Bryan with the greatest potential for policy-making, allowing him to combine the status of party leader with that of chief diplomat. When he took office, he told the press that he would guide his actions by the tenets of anti-imperialism and the hope for international peace.

The new Secretary's most immediate concern was less with making foreign policy than with finding patronage positions for thousands of his loyal supporters. While the State Department offered few opportunities for patronage, Bryan made the maximum use of those it presented. As a leader of the Nebraska party, he expected a major role in naming federal officeholders there. He found that Senator Gilbert Hitchcock held similar expectations. The battle over appointments in Nebraska raged throughout Bryan's tenure in the Cabinet; Wilson's best efforts failed to reconcile Bryan and Hitchcock. Other federal departments held possibilities for appointments, and Bryan asked fellow Cabinet members to help him reward as many supporters as possible. Packing federal offices with "deserving Democrats" (Bryan's phrase) caused the Commoner no embarrassment; he would probably have approved wholeheartedly the comment by Vice-President Thomas Marshall that "any office under the government that a Democrat can't fill . . . should be abolished." For Bryan, rewarding "deserving Democrats" was not a political chore. It was a pleasure, and he plunged into it with gusto, taking time for consideration of applicants even during international crises.

Within a few weeks of taking office, the new administration faced a potential crisis that combined domestic politics and international relations, exactly the combination for which Bryan felt best suited. The California legislature, led by Governor Hiram Johnson (who had been Theodore Roosevelt's running mate in 1912), seemed likely to pass legislation prohibiting persons ineligible for citizenship from owning agricultural land. Californians needed no more direct language to know that the proposal took aim at Japanese immigrants, who were prohibited by law from becoming naturalized citizens. Anti-Asian sentiment had long smoldered on the West Coast; on occasion it had burst into flames.

Previously, when Californians had threatened to pass anti-Japanese measures, pressures from national Republican leaders on local Republicans had usually sufficed to prevent passage. Now that the national administration came from the other party, Hiram Johnson seemed unwilling to help maintain friendly relations with the rising industrial power across the Pacific.

Sutemi Chinda, the Japanese Ambassador, made clear to Wilson and Bryan that his government looked with great disfavor upon legislation singling out Japanese for discriminatory treatment. Bryan accepted a Cabinet decision that he should go to California, address the legislature, and plead that they refrain from discriminating against the Japanese. Bryan considered his California trip potentially "the most thankless task I ever undertook." But he spoke to the legislature, seeking modifications in the pending legislation. While the few Democrats in the legislature followed Bryan's lead, the Progressive and Republican majority followed Johnson instead. Bryan knew that his trip had not changed the Californians' determination to enact discriminatory legislation, but he hoped that the Japanese government appreciated the gesture. When Japan insisted that the Wilson administration should declare the law invalid, some American military officers began to discuss preparations for war in the Pacific.

Bryan and Wilson quickly spiked such talk, depending on diplomacy to smooth over the crisis. A tense Chinda called upon Bryan in mid-May to ask for federal action to remove the blot on the honor of his people. Bryan tried to convey the friendliness of the American government, but he could not offer federal intervention. Chinda rose, saying, "I suppose, Mr. Secretary, this decision is final." Bryan also stood, but he extended his hand, flashed his broad smile, and replied, "There is nothing final between friends." Chinda resumed his seat and the discussion continued. Nonetheless, Bryan could not offer what the Japanese government wanted; his states' rights scruples, principles shared by Wilson and the Cabinet, prevented action against California. In the end, Bryan managed to keep relations with Japan from reaching the boiling point, even though he could find no way of cooling them.

The early months of the Wilson administration brought a number of other and more satisfying accomplishments. In April, Bryan carried out the pleasant task of confirming that the Seventeenth Amendment, providing for direct election of senators, had secured the necessary ratifications to become part of the Constitution. Throughout spring and summer, Congress worked on two major pieces of legislation of great interest to him: a revision of the tariff and a bill dealing with currency and banking matters.

Bryan had begun his political career as an advocate of tariff revision and had first captured national headlines with a speech against the protective tariff. The five national platforms he had helped to draft had all called for removal of high tariff rates. Two years before, the Democratic majority in the House of Representatives had tried to cut the tariff, but had become snarled in intra-party disputes. Bryan's first disillusionment with Champ Clark came when the Speaker refused to exert the leadership Bryan urged. Now the problem recurred. A few Democrats wanted to protect products from their states, notably sugar and wool. Wilson put pressure on the committee drafting the tariff bill, and the bill remained true to principle. Accompanying the tariff revision came another measure on which Bryan had cut his political eyeteeth: the income tax. Bryan had worked diligently for approval of the 16th Amendment to the Constitution, permitting the taxing of incomes. He took pleasure in the prompt implementation of the new measure, even though initial rates were low. Some Senators argued for a more progressive tax structure and for an inheritance tax, but Bryan defended the bill as a reasonable beginning.

Bryan involved himself only occasionally in the struggle for tariff reform and the income tax; he took a larger part in the creation of the Federal Reserve System. Virtually every-

one familiar with the economy agreed that a change in federal banking and monetary policy was inevitable, but wide
disagreement existed on the appropriate features for a new
policy. During the Taft administration, Congress had created a commission to study the banking system. Headed by
Senator Nelson W. Aldrich, a conservative Republican, the
commission recommended creation of a National Reserve
Association, essentially a central bank, controlled by bankers,
legally responsible for issuing the nation's currency and
holding government deposits, and capable of giving central
direction to the nation's banking and monetary systems.
Shocked progressives viewed the plan as giving government
sanction to Wall Street's control of money, and the plan had,
in fact, come from the pen of a prominent Wall Street finan-
cier. Some Democrats, such as Congressman Carter Glass of
the House Banking Committee, accepted many features of
the Aldrich plan, but sought to decentralize it by creating a
number of regional reserve institutions rather than a central
bank. Bryan and his followers insisted that control of any
reserve ought to rest with the government, not the bankers;
they insisted as well that issuing currency ought to be a function of the government, not of banks. With no strongly defined position of his own, Wilson tried to act as mediator
among various factions of his party.

Wilson understood the influence Bryan enjoyed with key
members of the House and Senate, and the central significance he gave to banking and monetary policy. The president sought his advice and support both through intermedi-
aries and directly. When Bryan met with Wilson, he outlined
his objections to the Glass proposal and repeated his views
that currency should be issued by the government, and that
the government should control the reserve bank. Bryan cautioned that presidential support for the Glass bill would deeply divide the party and would endanger the pending tariff
bill. He adduced Jefferson, Jackson, and all the recent party
platforms in support of his stand, made clear that he could

not support the Glass proposal, and suggested that he would quietly resign if Wilson pursued a course at variance with the party's platforms. Wilson finally agreed to Bryan's demands; the Glass bill was amended so that Bryan could support it.

Even after Bryan fell in line, the modified version of the bill faced opposition from Bryanite members of Congress who wanted to add provisions to assist farmers or to limit the power of bankers. Wilson made a few concessions to those concerned for agricultural credits and to those worried about interlocking directorates in banking. Bryan finally had to disavow those who continued to push for more extreme changes, and to urge the Democratic caucus to support the president's wishes. Senate Democrats amended the measure to create a deposit insurance fund, a concept modeled after the Oklahoma and Nebraska laws, and in fulfillment of the 1908 platform; that section disappeared when the conference committee reconciled the differences between the Senate and House versions. Surrounded by the entire Cabinet and Democratic Congressional leaders, Wilson signed the measure in late December. Bryan had played a central role in the formulation and passage of the most significant piece of domestic legislation of the Wilson administration.

VII

Crusades for Peace

WILLIAM JENNINGS BRYAN, the nation's fortieth secretary of state, fulfilled few of the usual expectations for his
office. European nations typically staffed their foreign minis-
tries with members of the aristocracy; many of Bryan's predecessors came from social backgrounds that allowed them to
meet titled ambassadors without a faux pas. Bryan, the arch-
democrat, cared little for protocol and formality, considering
them relics of monarchy. His desk at the State Department
usually looked as cluttered as his desk at Fairview. Bryan had
never given much attention to his personal appearance; Mary
now inspected him each morning to be certain that his shave
passed muster. On hot summer days, he took off his coat and
collar and greeted visitors in his shirt sleeves, palm fan waving. Even though he served grape juice and mineral water at
state banquets, his favorite drink was water. Radishes remained his favorite snack. With his bald dome, portly build,
and baggy trousers, Bryan looked more like a small-town editor than an international diplomat.

Many years before, at the age of nineteen, Will Bryan had
written to a friend that "in a few years it will not be necessary
to shoot a man to convince him that you are right and to blot
out a nation to prove to them that their principles are false."
The optimism of the nineteen-year-old remained deeply im-
bedded in the middle-aged secretary of state. Beginning in
1904, Bryan frequently delivered "The Prince of Peace," a
speech he considered among his best. While he presented the

peace of Christ as primarily individual, he also pointed to international implications. Individual peace came from "faith in God and trust in an overruling Providence," and from the assurance of immortality that faith produced. Peace within and peace with others, Bryan proclaimed, took the form of overcoming evil through good, of living "an

Mary Baird Bryan watching Secretary of State William Jennings Bryan signing conciliation treaties with France, Great Britain, Spain, and China, September 15, 1914. Bryan considered this day especially momentous because the nations represented accounted for well over half the population of the world. (Photograph courtesy of the Nebraska State Historical Society.)

upright life." The peace of which Bryan spoke extended as well to nations: "The Gospel of the Prince of Peace gives us the only hope that the world has—and it is an increasing hope—of the substitution of reason for the arbitrament of force in the settlement of international disputes. And our nation ought not to wait for other nations—it ought to take the lead and prove its faith in the omnipotence of truth."

Bryan had not limited his advocacy of peace to the Chautauqua circuit, nor to peripheral references in speeches dealing largely with other topics. Beginning with his world tour of 1905–1906, he increasingly addressed himself directly to the subject of international understanding. In a major speech in 1910, he denied that armaments brought peace and condemned the "profitable patriotism" that sought contracts to build ever more and bigger battleships. He closed his address by repeating an appeal, first made in *The Commoner* in early 1905, for the United States to take the lead in proposing treaties with every nation, pledging to submit to "an impartial tribunal" any dispute that could not be resolved through normal diplomacy. The tribunal would make findings of fact that would then provide the basis for settling the dispute. He insisted that *all* questions, even those involving national honor, could be resolved in that fashion. "Whenever a nation wants to go to war," Bryan said, "no matter what the subject is, it turns it into a question of national honor and goes to shooting." His proposal, he believed, would allow nations to separate fact from honor, and "when the questions of fact are settled, we would generally find there was no real question of honor."

Bryan's confidence that rational discourse would soon replace war put him into a large and influential company during the early years of the twentieth century. The years from 1899 to 1914 mark the zenith of the international arbitration movement, and of the peace movement more generally. While some argued that the technology of destruction had developed to the point where modern war could produce no winners, others attempted to develop mechanisms for the resolution of international disputes without recourse to conflict. Businessmen such as Andrew Carnegie contributed generously to the cause, and voluntary organizations took up the same theme. An international conference in 1899 created a Permanent Court of Arbitration. Located in the Netherlands and usually called the Hague Court, it consisted of a panel from which disputing nations might select arbitrators.

Theodore Roosevelt's secretary of state, John Hay, had drawn up a number of bilateral treaties in each of which the United States and the other nations agreed to use the Hague Court for the resolution of differences not involving "the vital interests, the independence, or the honor" of the two. The Senate balked at accepting the treaties unless they included a provision allowing the Senate to pass individually on each matter submitted to arbitration. Hay's successor, Elihu Root, obtained nearly two dozen treaties containing the Senate's stipulation during the years 1908 and 1909. Bryan urged President Taft to accept even questions of "honor" as proper subjects for arbitration, and in 1911, Taft's secretary of state negotiated arbitration treaties with Great Britain and France covering all "justiciable" questions. The Senate amended the treaties so extensively that Taft set them aside as hopeless.

When Bryan took office as secretary of state, he wasted no time in presenting his plan for conciliation treaties. In April 1913, he wrote a memorandum outlining his proposal. "The parties hereto agree," the draft began, "that all questions of every character and nature whatever, in dispute between them, shall, when diplomatic efforts fail, be submitted for investigation and report to an international commission." The Cabinet discussed the idea and modified some of its details. He then took the draft to the Senate Foreign Relations Committee to secure its approval of the principle; he wanted no repetition of the fate of the Taft arbitration treaties. On April 24, 1913, the State Department submitted the final version to the forty nations maintaining diplomatic relations with the United States under the heading of "President Wilson's Peace Proposal." A supplementary memorandum from Bryan proposed details such as the composition of the commission, the length of time for investigation, and a freeze on military and naval expansion during the period of investigation.

Negotiations resulting from Bryan's initiative eventually produced thirty treaties, varying somewhat in detail, but all embracing the central feature of a "cooling off" period, typically a year, during which the parties agreed not to go to war and, instead, to seek outside fact-finding in the event of any dispute they could not resolve through normal diplomatic means. The thirty nations that signed included all the Latin American nations but Mexico and Colombia, and nearly all the nations of Europe. Of the major powers, only Japan, Germany, Austria-Hungary, and Turkey did not sign one of Bryan's treaties. Bryan considered these thirty treaties the most significant accomplishment of his term in the State Department, containing "the basis of an enduring peace."

During the summer of 1914, Bryan ordered some old swords melted down and cast into miniature plow-shaped paperweights, each inscribed with the Biblical injunction, "THEY SHALL BEAT THEIR SWORDS INTO PLOW-SHARES," and with two of Bryan's own epigrams, "NOTHING IS FINAL BETWEEN FRIENDS," and "DIPLOMACY IS THE ART OF KEEPING COOL." He presented these souvenirs to each of the diplomats with whom he had worked on a treaty and to the president and each member of the Cabinet. When it came time to commission an official portrait for the State Department, Bryan made certain that the artist painted him with a conciliation treaty in his hand. Not everyone shared his faith that his treaties could prevent war. Theodore Roosevelt thought them fatuous, and some European diplomats considered them irrelevant. The *New York Times* acknowledged grudgingly only that they "can do no possible harm and may do much good."

Colombia had not joined in the conciliation treaties because of long-standing antagonism stemming from the catalytic role of the United States in the secession of Panama. When the Colombian minister proposed to Bryan, in early May 1913, that the two nations submit their differences to the Hague Court, Bryan suggested negotiations. Wilson personally drafted directions to the American representative in Colombia. Discussions quickly produced agreement. The first article of the treaty set its tone: "The Government of the United States . . . expresses, in its own name and in the name of the people of the United States, sincere regret that anything should have occurred to interrupt or to mar the relations of cordial friendship that had so long subsisted between the two nations." The treaty then promised Colombia $25 million in settlement of Colombian claims against the United States.

The agreement practically reduced Theodore Roosevelt to apoplexy. The actions for which the treaty apologized could only refer to his role in the Panamanian revolt. Bryan strongly urged ratification of the treaty, arguing that "friendships cannot rest upon force." Opposition in the Senate kept the treaty from coming to a vote, however, and it never took effect. Despite Senate rejection, the initiative displayed by Bryan and Wilson went far toward convincing Latin American nations that the day of the "Big Stick" had ended.

Theodore Roosevelt created the "Big Stick" metaphor in 1901 when he defined his approach to Latin America as, "Speak softly and carry a big stick." In 1901, he approved the creation of protectorate status for Cuba. Cuba became independent in 1902 only after accepting constitutional provisions to permit the United States to intervene in its affairs and to prohibit a foreign policy at variance with American interests. Soon after, when Colombia balked at signing a treaty giving the United States rights to build a canal across its territory in Panama, Roosevelt encouraged revolution there and later boasted, "I took the canal zone and let Congress debate." The treaty he negotiated with the new republic of Panama made that nation a second protectorate. In 1905, Roosevelt took control of the collection of customs, the major source of revenue, in the Dominican Republic in order to guarantee that nation's ability to pay off its debts. The "Big Stick" in practice meant American hegemony in the Caribbean and in Central America. Bryan thought that Roosevelt's "Big Stick" metaphor betokened a failure of statesmanship. "The man who speaks softly," Bryan later wrote, "does not need a big stick; and, if he yields to temptation and equips himself with one, the tone of his voice is very likely to change."

When Bryan became secretary of state, he found a recently negotiated treaty between Nicaragua and the United States awaiting Senate action. He withdrew the treaty and renegotiated some of its features. The original document had provided that the United States would pay Nicaragua $3 million in return for a long-term lease on two islands in the Caribbean, the right to build a naval base on Nicaraguan soil, and a permanent option on an isthmian canal route through Nicaragua. The treaty specified that the money would go to retire debts owed American bankers. Bryan investigated the financial status of Nicaragua and sought to change the treaty so that Nicaragua might be relieved of its obligations to American bankers through a direct loan from the American government. The $3 million might then be used for "education or permanent public works." Unfortunately for Bryan's altruism, Wilson disagreed. In addition, the Nicaraguans convinced the State Department to add provisions to the treaty making their nation a protectorate. Bryan voiced no objections. Members of his party in Congress found these provisions troublesome and steered Bryan back to anti-imperialist principles. The renegotiated document, remembered as the Bryan-Chamorro Treaty, made few changes from the initial draft Bryan had found so objectionable.

Elsewhere in the area, Bryan found that both Haiti and the Dominican Republic demanded attention. The American minister to the Dominican Republic, James Sullivan, had come with strong recommendations from Wilson's secretary, Joseph Tumulty; Bryan felt some doubts, but acquiesced in Sullivan's appointment and relied upon him for information. Sullivan soon entered into machinations with the Dominican President to secure favors for his cousin and probably for himself. When revolution broke out, Sullivan fed Bryan and Wilson misleading information until the nation teetered on the verge of collapse. Wilson removed Sullivan and arranged for elections to be supervised by the United States. Bryan's intent for the Dominican Republic had been the same as for Nicaragua, the freeing of the nation from thralldom to foreign bankers, but the result was increased American intervention. A similar pattern developed in Haiti. Throughout his tenure as secretary of state, Bryan held off State Department career officials who wanted to establish an outright protectorate in Haiti. Marines landed in Haiti a few months after Bryan resigned from the State Department. In the end, the Wilson administration gave in completely to the advocates of the "Big Stick." The United States intervened more in the affairs of Caribbean and Central American nations between 1913 and 1921 than during any comparable eight-year period.

Events in Mexico severely tested Bryan's commitment to peace and to understanding reached through reason. In 1911, Francisco Madero had overthrown the thirty-four-year-old regime of Porfirio Diaz; the inchoate movement Madero symbolized posed a threat to the power of the great landholders, the church, and the military. Shortly before Wilson and Bryan took office, General Victoriano Huerta toppled Madero's government, killed Madero, and sought American recognition. Taft did nothing, leaving the problem for Wilson and Bryan. Huerta soon gained a reputation as brutal and dissolute. Several Mexican state governors refused to acknowledge his regime as legitimate, and opposition to him coalesced around Venustiano Carranza. American businesses with interests in Mexico urged support for the Huerta government, but Wilson and Bryan shared a disgust with the means by which he had achieved power. Neither man saw a pressing need for immediate recognition. Bryan later recalled: "I was so unaccustomed to the consideration of public questions separated from both morals and the principle of popular government that I was not able to endorse the position of those who favored the recognition of Huerta." Diplomatic recognition usually signified neither approval nor disapproval of a government; it meant only that the nation granting recognition considered the recipient to be exercising the functions of government. By refusing recognition, Wilson and Bryan added a policy dimension, making clear their distaste for the method by which Huerta took power and signaling their sympathies for his opponents.

On July 19, 1913, Bryan sent Wilson a long memorandum on the Mexican situation. He outlined a series of steps that might restore popularly elected government and protect Americans in Mexico, but he counseled against military intervention "to protect property which Americans are not willing to leave." If the United States should intervene in Mexico to protect American investments, Bryan argued, it would sink to "a level with those nations which have extended their territory by conquest, first allowing their citizens to go abroad in quest of gain and then sending an army to guarantee the profits sought." He also feared that any military action would cause an "immeasurable loss of prestige," which would prevent the United States from exercising its proper role as "the leader in the peace movement and as the exponent of human rights."

After several months of watchful waiting, Bryan drafted a message to the major European powers asking them to withhold recognition of the Huerta government on the grounds that the United States was unwilling "to have an

American Republic exploited by the commercial interests of our own or any other country through a government resting on force." State Department Counselor John Bassett Moore, a leading expert on international law, persuaded Wilson and Bryan not to send the message, but Wilson incorporated some of its concepts into a speech in Mobile, Alabama, in late October. In his Mobile speech, Wilson attached such moral dimensions to recognition that his approach has sometimes been labeled "missionary diplomacy." Bryan applauded the Mobile announcement and urged Wilson to expand it into a new Monroe Doctrine. "The right of American republics to work out their own destiny along lines consistent with popular government," Bryan wrote, "is just as much menaced today by foreign financial interests as it was a century ago by the political aspirations of foreign governments."

Wilson and Bryan continued to watch and wait until early in 1914, when an incident at Tampico finally led to intervention. A group of American naval personnel went ashore to buy gasoline; Mexican officials detained them, marched them through the streets, then released them. The Mexican officer apologized for the inconvenience, but the American naval officer in charge demanded a twenty-one gun salute to the American flag as well. This demand, rapidly conveyed to Washington and Mexico City, met with approval from Wilson, Bryan, and Secretary of the Navy Josephus Daniels, Bryan's closest ally in the Cabinet. Huerta suggested that the episode be submitted to the Hague Court for fact-finding; Bryan rejected the offer and reiterated the initial demand. When Wilson took an even harsher line than Bryan, he dutifully backed the President. Finally, Wilson determined to occupy the city of Veracruz to prevent the landing of weapons and, more importantly, to cut Huerta off from customs revenues. Hope for peaceful resolution had ended. Military intervention began. Bryan acquiesced. Denied the revenues of the Veracruz customshouse, Huerta abdicated within three months, and Carranza soon assumed power. Bryan hoped that the administration's policies were to be vindicated, but he soon found the anti-Huerta forces dissolving into competing factions. Mexico broke down into chaos and bloody civil war. Bryan must have shared Wilson's sense that "the situation has become so complicated that I feel that I have lost the threads of it." There matters remained when Bryan resigned from the State Department.

By any measure, the Wilson-Bryan policy for Mexico had failed. Huerta's regime had toppled, but at the cost of intervention only a step removed from war. The fall of Huerta had not brought the popularly elected, reformist government both Bryan and Wilson had envisioned. As in Nicaragua and the Caribbean, Bryan found himself following the lead of others, ultimately ignoring his own first principles, and behaving exactly as he had accused policy-makers only a few years before: "Whenever a nation wants to go to war, no matter what the subject is, it turns it into a question of national honor and goes to shooting." In the Tampico incident, a naval officer had turned a minor incident into "a question of national honor"; the Wilson administration accepted the definition because it presented an excuse for military intervention.

Although Bryan failed to translate his hopes for Latin America into policy, he had somewhat more success with another of his longstanding causes. From 1900 through 1912, long after most politicians had pushed the Philippine Islands from their thoughts, Bryan continued to write into his party's platforms a demand for the islands' independence. As secretary of state, he wanted to translate this longtime commitment into policy, but initially he found Wilson unenthusiastic. Eventually, the Commoner succeeded in dispelling the president's misgivings and in winning presidential support for the Jones Bill, which finally passed in 1916. The act promised independence in its preamble, although it contained no specific provisions or timetables for transfer of authority.

At the same time that Bryan's attention was fixed on Mexico's plunge into civil war, the nations of Europe were executing diplomatic and military maneuvers that were to take them beyond sanity and propel them into five years of carnage. Over the previous dozen years, nations had shuffled and reshuffled alliances and ententes until two major power centers emerged; Germany, Austria-Hungary, and Italy formed one, and Britain, France, and Russia composed another. The assassination of the heir to the Austro-Hungarian throne by a Serbian nationalist in June 1914 led to Austrian demands on Serbia a month later, then to declaration of war. When Russia mobilized its army in support of Serbia, Germany (Austria-Hungary's ally) declared war on Russia and then on France, Russia's ally. Belgium refused to grant Germany permission to cross its territory, so Germany declared war on that small nation, prompting Britain to enter the widening vortex of conflict. Eventually, Bulgaria joined Germany, Austria-Hungary, and Turkey to form the Central Powers. Italy, Rumania, and Japan sided with Britain, France, and Russia and became known as the Allies. The events of August 1914 crushed the optimism of many who had come to believe that reason had replaced force in world affairs. Yet Bryan refused to lose hope. "It may be," he suggested in October, "that the world needed one more awful object lesson to prove conclusively the fallacy of the doctrine that preparedness for war can give assurance of peace."

With the war came crucial decisions for the American government. Virtually no one advocated entrance into the war, but problems immediately arose in defining neutrality. Bryan prepared most early statements, although Wilson usually looked them over before they were issued. When France asked J.P. Morgan for help in borrowing money in the United States, Bryan defined loans from American bankers to belligerent nations as incompatible with neutrality. "Money," he declared soon after in *The Commoner*, "is the worst of contrabands—it commands all other things." Robert

Lansing, who succeeded John Bassett Moore as State Department Counselor, suggested to Bryan the need for a
presidential address to the nation on the need for neutral
behavior; Bryan forwarded the suggestion with some slight
changes and his full support. The president accordingly appealed to the nation "to be neutral in fact as well as in
name . . . impartial in thought as well as in action." At the
beginning, Wilson and Bryan saw eye to eye on the need to
keep American interests separate from those of either side
in the European conflict.

While Bryan and Wilson agreed that the United States
should not become a belligerent, they soon parted company
on the best means of maintaining neutrality. For Bryan, neutrality took priority over all other concerns, and avoiding
any pretext for involvement took priority over neutral
rights. Because he recognized that the danger of American
involvement increased with every month the war lasted, he
also sought ways to bring the conflict to an end. Wilson, too,
hoped to avoid American belligerency, but as the war
dragged on, he increasingly emphasized neutral rights, a
posture beneficial primarily to the Allies. Within six weeks of
Bryan's definition of loans as "the worst of contrabands,"
Wilson was writing to Lansing that he would not oppose the
extension of "credits" to belligerents by American banking
firms. Although no one could distinguish between a "credit"
and a "loan," Bryan announced that the State Department
would not object to the extension of massive credits by
American bankers to the French government.

Bryan hoped from the beginning that the United States
might be able to bring the belligerents to a conference table.
In September 1914, when the German ambassador seemed
to indicate interest in American mediation, Bryan sounded
out the British and French. The effort came to nothing, so
he urged Wilson to ask both sides to talk peace. Wilson had
begun to rely on Colonel House for advice more than on
Bryan, and House reinforced Wilson's sentiments that he

should make no offer to mediate until asked by the belligerents. In late 1914, when the German ambassador suggested the possibility of American mediation, House presented himself to Wilson as the best emissary. He also pressed upon Wilson his view that Bryan was "unfitted" for "such a delicate mission." Wilson accepted that reasoning, and House left for Europe in late January 1915. From the beginning, House made clear to the British that he sympathized with their position and would do nothing to embarrass them.

In command of the seas during the opening months of the war, Britain had established a distant blockade of German ports and had greatly lengthened the list of contraband goods. At the time of the British pronouncement, Bryan was on the hustings for his party, seeking to hold Democratic Congressional majorities against the usual tendency for the party in the White House to lose seats at midterm elections. During Bryan's absence, Lansing became acting secretary of state for more than a month. He proved willing, not just to modify Bryan's opposition to loans, but also to submit to British restrictions on neutral trade. Early in 1915, Britain declared food to be contraband and ordered that ships carrying food should not enter either German ports or neutral ports from which cargoes might be sent to Germany. Germany responded with a blockade of the British Isles, to be enforced by the submarine, its new and frightening weapon. Germany also announced that neutral ships within the blockade area would be endangered because of the British practice of disguising their vessels with neutral flags. This action, Germany insisted, came because of British efforts to starve German citizens, combatants and non-combatants alike. Wilson acquiesced in British contraband definitions, though they went far beyond those usually accepted in international law. Now, however, he took a firm posture toward Germany. Although he drafted the protest note to Germany, he discussed it with Bryan and it went out over the Secretary's signature. Wilson's note asked Germany to reconsider its decision to employ submarine warfare. The United States, warned the note, would hold Germany to "strict accountability" for its actions and would take whatever steps might be necessary "to safeguard American lives and property and to secure to American citizens the full enjoyment of their acknowledged rights on the high seas."

The inevitable did not happen until late March, when a German submarine torpedoed the British ship *Falaba* and an American drowned. Bryan urged restraint in drafting a protest. He pointed out that Germany had warned Americans to avoid British ships, that Britain continued to use the American flag to disguise its ships, and that the United States seemed to attach more significance to the drowning of "a few people" than to "starving a nation." Bryan wanted to warn American citizens to avoid travel on British vessels traversing the war zone. He also urged Wilson to launch a public initiative to bring the belligerents to the conference table.

The president pondered the nature of the protest note for nearly a month following the sinking, but then leaned to Lansing's hard line rather than Bryan's course. Bryan remonstrated at length, indicating his fears that the president's approach would "inflame the already hostile feeling against us in Germany." He protested what seemed the quite different policies toward Germany and toward Britain, arguing that "denunciation of one and silence as to the other will be construed by some as partiality." He pointed out that Wilson seemed to be implying "the right of a citizen to involve his country in war when by exercising ordinary care he could have avoided danger." Wilson responded, "I am not at all confident that we are on the right track in considering such a note as I outlined," and he wearily suggested that "perhaps it is not necessary to make formal representations in the matter at all." He turned down Bryan's proposals for a public call for a peace conference as unlikely to produce results, but before he reached a decision on the proper response to the *Falaba* situation, all Americans had their attention distracted by the sinking of the *Lusitania* and the drowning of 1,198 passengers, among them 128 Americans.

Before the *Lusitania* sailed, the German Embassy had placed an advertisement in American newspapers warning travellers that "vessels flying the flag of Great Britain, or any of her allies, are liable to destruction." Bryan thought the notice a positive sign; Lansing found it "insolent." Soon after Bryan learned of the loss of the ship, he told Mary of his suspicion that "England has been using our citizens to protect her ammunition!" When his suspicions were confirmed, he compared the shipping of munitions on a passenger vessel to "putting women and children in front of an army," and strongly urged restraint in drafting a message to Germany. Bryan pushed the president to propose arbitration, suggested coupling any protest to Germany with one to Britain, and argued strongly that American citizens ought not be allowed to drag the nation into war because they risked their lives by traveling on a belligerent vessel in a war zone. Lansing wanted a strong response to Germany based on the rights of neutrals and reiterating the "strict accountability" threat of the earlier message. Bryan saw such a course as giving Germany the decision for American entrance into the war: if Germany refused to halt its submarine campaign, "strict accountability" could only mean American belligerency. Wilson's draft leaned more to Lansing's views than Bryan's and appealed to Germany to end its submarine attacks. Citing Lansing's advice, Wilson refused Bryan's request to notify American citizens to avoid travel on belligerent ships. After initially agreeing that a protest to Britain would be in order, Wilson conferred with other advisers, then changed his mind. All the same, Wilson assured Bryan that he had been "deeply moved" by his arguments. Bryan continued to press for moderation in the language of the message, and won what he considered to be important concessions.

In discussions with the American ambassador in Berlin, a

German official claimed that Bryan had told Constantin Dumba, Austria's ambassador in Washington, that the *Lusitania* note was but a "sop to public opinion," and that the German government could discount it. In fact, neither Dumba nor Bryan had said anything of the sort, but the conversation, as reported to Washington, further weakened Bryan's already tenuous position. The German response to the *Lusitania* note provided little satisfaction. The Cabinet meeting of June 1 witnessed a discussion of means to secure a German concession. Seemingly under severe tension, Bryan first held back, then lashed out that the Cabinet seemed to favor the Allies. Wilson reprimanded him for the outburst, but on the next day, he asked Bryan for assistance in drafting the reply to Germany, adding "that I very much need all the counsel I can get, and I shall, of course, chiefly value yours."

Bryan's memorandum recapitulated all that he had previously offered the president. Wilson also solicited advice from Lansing, then composed his own draft of a note. On June 4 the cabinet met to consider the matter. When Bryan realized he could not convince Wilson to initiate arbitration or to limit American travel, he concluded that he could not sign the second *Lusitania* note. He informed Wilson at the end of the Cabinet meeting that he intended to resign, then he sent a final written appeal to the president, asking support for a law prohibiting passenger ships from carrying munitions, a note to Germany emphasizing arbitration, and a strong protest to Britain over its restriction of American trade. After spending Sunday in the country considering his decision, he met with the president. House later quoted Wilson as reporting that Bryan said, "Colonel House has been Secretary of State, not I, and I have never had your full confidence." Bryan came home from his session with Wilson on the verge of complete physical collapse. Grace and Mary assisted him to a sofa and he told them, "We have come to the parting of the ways." He wrote his letter of resignation and sent it to the White House. The family sat down to dinner but could say or eat little. Finally, Mary rushed from the table, locked herself in her room, and—for the only time in Grace's memory—broke down sobbing.

The resignation must actually have come as something of a relief to Bryan, for his twenty-seven months in the State Department had proven difficult. For the first time in many years, he had kept regular hours in an office. His own work ethic and strong sense of responsibility meant that he put in long hours, arriving in the early morning, staying late, taking work home for the evening, and usually putting in a full Saturday. Only the Sabbath remained free of State Department obligations. For the first time since the 1904 convention, Bryan's health began to impose limitations on his activities; in March 1914, his doctor diagnosed him as diabetic and placed him on a strict diet to control the ailment.

The State Department position not only imposed a more rigorous work schedule than had been Bryan's wont, but it also limited his income. Throughout the years since 1896, Bryan had earned most of his income through summer and winter lecture tours, supplemented by royalties from his books and by *The Commoner*. The salary appropriated for the secretary of state fell far below his lecture tour earnings; his obligations to church, charity, and insurance companies ate up more than half his official salary. In addition, the Bryans had begun to improve land they owned in Florida, building a home eventually called Villa Serena; they spent the summers in rented quarters in Asheville, North Carolina. To all these expenses were added the cost of renting a home in Washington and staffing it with the servants necessary for proper diplomatic entertaining. To meet these obligations, Bryan received permission from Wilson to continue his practice of Chautauqua lecturing; to compensate for time away from the State Department, he allowed himself no vacations. In all, he spent more time on duty than his immediate predecessors, but he nonetheless came under harsh criticism, mostly from Republicans, for demeaning his office by lecturing for pay and for being so greedy as to forsake his duties for the Chautauqua circuit. Other criticism, most of it also from Republicans, stemmed from his preoccupation with the placement of "deserving Democrats."

The press responded to Bryan's resignation with a hail of abuse. One New York paper called it "a sorry service to his country," another accused him of deserting the president, and the ever-hostile *Times* called it "the wisest act of his political career." With few exceptions, national press opinion echoed the vituperation. Bryan's mail, however, brought a deluge of letters supporting his action. The people of New York seemed far more supportive than the city's newspapers; when Bryan spoke there in late June, seventy thousand came to listen and applaud. In Lincoln, six thousand turned out to hear their fellow townsman defend his course. Bryan told the Lincolnites how fortunate they were in having the Allegheny Mountains between them and New York, to "serve as a dike to keep the prejudice, the venom, the insolence, and the ignorance of the New York press from inundating the Mississippi Valley." While he defended his actions, he offered no criticism of Wilson. Throughout the months to come, he always maintained that they were both seeking peace, but from different perspectives. The Bryans traveled to San Francisco in July, where W.J. addressed a crowd estimated at 100,000. "The world," he said, "has run mad," and he urged the United States to look "toward better things than war." Throughout the remainder of 1915, he spoke across the nation, often on foreign policy and against the military and naval buildup being urged in Washington, but other times in support of prohibition or his lastest cause, woman suffrage. During the months when Fairview lay under a blanket of snow, the Bryans lived in their new Florida home, surrounded by palms and bougainvillea; each day W.J. enjoyed working out for several hours by felling trees and cutting wood.

Throughout the early months of 1916, as Germany finally promised to abandon unrestricted submarine warfare, Bryan opposed efforts to increase military and naval expenditures. "Preparedness," he argued, "provokes war." Increased military and naval expenditures, he said, could only be secured by creating fear; fear then became hatred, which prevented rational efforts at understanding. All the while, "every contractor, battleship builder, and manufacturer of munitions of war applauds." The war in Europe amply demonstrated that preparedness could not prevent war. "We dare not trust the peace of the world to those who spend their time in getting ready for wars that should never come," he said. "Half the energy employed in preparing for war would effectually prevent war if used in propagating the principles which make for peace." In late August 1916, Bryan took some satisfaction in the increased income tax imposed to pay for a large navy appropriations measure, and in efforts by Congressional progressives to take profits out of preparedness. He also took satisfaction in the strong response to his efforts and those of others seeking to prevent American involvement in the war in Europe.

Earlier in 1916, Bryan had launched a campaign to rid the Nebraska Democratic party of the "saloon-picked, brewery-branded crowd," and predicted that a month's campaign would suffice. Despite this optimism, Nebraska Democrats again rejected the Bryans' effort to make them drink water. His brother Charles failed to win the Democratic nomination for governor; W.J. lost his bid to be elected a delegate to the presidential nominating convention. For the first time in twenty years, a national Democratic convention opened without Bryan as either a delegate or as a candidate. He did attend, but as a reporter. Wilson wanted the keynote of the convention to be "Americanism," but the delegates took their cue from keynote speaker Martin Glynn, who found that the strongest response came from emphasizing that Wilson had kept the nation out of the war.

Bryan provoked the usual demonstrations of support whenever he appeared in the convention's press section; he finally resorted to hiding under the platform to avoid disrupting the proceedings. Once Wilson won renomination, Bryan yielded to the clamor and spoke to the convention. He spent more than an hour praising Wilson because of his domestic reforms and because he "does not want this nation plunged into war." At the close of his address, every delegate in the hall came forward to shake his hand.

Bryan carried his support for the Democratic ticket into the fall campaign, filling numerous speaking commitments, especially in the West. The outcome hung by a thread, but Wilson won with 49.4 percent of the popular vote. He carried the South, Ohio, and nearly every Western state; Bryan's speaking engagements had been concentrated in those Western states that gave Wilson his victory. Not only could Bryan claim a major share in Wilson's victory, but he could also take great satisfaction in those states that adopted prohibition: Michigan, South Dakota, Montana, and—closest to his heart—Nebraska. More than half the states had now banned the saloon, and national prohibition seemed increasingly possible.

After the election, Bryan resumed his efforts against preparedness, for peace, for prohibition, and for woman suffrage. Wilson finally yielded to one of the Commoner's most persistent suggestions, that the president try to arrange a peace conference and that he seek statements from each belligerent defining its war objectives. In late January 1917, however, Germany announced resumption of unrestricted submarine warfare. Wilson responded first by breaking diplomatic relations and urging Germany to reconsider. Bryan argued that the only safe course was to prevent Americans from traveling where the submarines operated. He called for a national referendum before any declaration of war, and he cooperated closely with Robert La Follette in opposing a Wilson proposal to arm American merchant ships.

Congress adjourned on March 4, but Wilson called it into special session on April 2 to ask for a declaration of war. After a lengthy debate, Congress complied by a vote of 373 to 50 in the House and 82 to 6 in the Senate. Wilson signed the declaration of war on April 6.

Bryan sadly wrote to Wilson, offering his services: "Please enroll me as a private whenever I am needed. . . . Until called to the colors I shall, through the Red Cross, contribute to the comfort of soldiers in the hospitals and, through the YMCA, aid in safeguarding the morals of the men in camp." Bryan intended his offer to serve as a private to be wholly metaphoric. Throughout the war he distributed copies of his plowshare paperweight.

The Bryans outside their Florida home, Villa Serena, December 1923. (Photograph courtesy of the Nebraska State Historical Society.)

VIII

The Final Battle: Crusade Against Evolution

FROM AUGUST 1914 TO APRIL 1917, Bryan held first rank among those seeking to prevent the United States from entering the turbulent maelstrom in Europe. Once war came, however, he offered to do what he could to assist the cause. To him, this represented neither contradiction nor reversal. When the nation had to decide either to enter the war or stay out, he opposed American participation in "the causeless war." Once Congress declared war, he again saw only two sides, the United States and the Central Powers. He felt no hesitation in choosing his side or in rearranging his priorities. The shortest route to peace was to win as quickly as possible.

Since some Americans would sacrifice their lives, Bryan had no doubts that others should contribute their wealth; he advocated that Congress enact steeply progressive income taxes and excess profits taxes to pay for the war, rather than burden future generations with its cost. Bryan also stood willing to sacrifice some civil liberties to further the war effort. "Whatever the government does is right," he announced. Criticism of the administration, he argued, only bred dissension, thereby delaying the victory that would bring peace. He drew the line in applying such a gag rule to members of the Congress, however, and he urged those critical of the war to write their complaints directly to Congress, rather than make public charges. Throughout the war, Bryan spoke extensively, promoting conservation of food and fuel, donations for the Red Cross and Y.M.C.A., and Liberty Bond sales. He reserved much of his attention for his three most important issues: peace, prohibition, and woman suffrage.

The drive to dry up the nation was approaching victory, and no one spent more hours on the lecture circuit in support than the former secretary of state, who had served diplomats grape juice instead of wine. By the mid-teens, Bryan had emerged as the nation's most prominent prohibitionist. In 1917, he spent hour after hour lobbying legislators whose votes held the balance when the House of Representatives voted on submission of the Eighteenth Amendment, which would prohibit manufacture, sale, or transportation of alcoholic beverages. During the House debate, Bryan acted as field marshal for the dry forces, watching from the gallery, sending directives to the floor leaders, and rounding up missing votes. The next step was ratification by thirty-six states, three-quarters of the total. The National Dry Federation, a coalition of nearly sixty organizations committed to the cold water reform, elected Bryan as its president in early 1918. With that backing, he carried the fight for ratification to state after state. He applauded when Congress enacted prohibition on a war-time, emergency basis in fall 1918, and took special pleasure in Nebraska's role as the thirty-sixth state to ratify the Eighteenth Amendment. Early in 1919, he attended ceremonies recording the ratification, and later that day received a testimonial from the National Dry Federation. Both opponents and supporters credited Bryan with having done more than any other individual to secure the success of the cold water reform.

Bryan had been reluctant to proclaim public support for woman suffrage when he assumed the Cabinet post in 1913. Soon, however, he said in public what he had previously reserved for private conversations, and in 1914 he campaigned, unsuccessfully, for passage of a suffrage amendment in Nebraska. He saw women, more than men, as powerful forces for peace and prohibition, but he feared that the prohibition issue might drag suffrage down to defeat. His analysis proved accurate for Nebraska in 1914, but by 1916 he thought prohibition might help the suffrage cause. He and Mary both spoke on behalf of the proposed constitutional amendment to extend the suffrage to women, and they joined in celebrating its approval in 1920.

The Bryan's efforts were interrupted in early 1919 when both required hospitalization. Mary had begun to experience pain and swelling in the joints of her hands, feet, and legs. W.J. accompanied her to Baltimore for tests. Her affliction, apparently arthritis, required braces and crutches for walking; eventually, it confined her to a wheelchair. Leaving Mary in Baltimore, W.J. went to Washington to consult his doctor for what he feared might be pneumonia. He soon received a diagnosis of facial erysipelas, a painful skin infection characterized by inflammation and fever; it confined him to bed for four weeks.

The war not only fulfilled Bryan's wishes for prohibition and woman suffrage, it also held out hope for another of his causes, public ownership of railroads. In December 1917, Wilson placed all railways under government control. Bryan saw the opportunity for what he had first proposed in 1904 and repeated in 1906—government ownership. He feared his proposal would be rejected as impractical, but he wrote to his brother Charles: "I have not in the past been deterred by fear of unpopularity from advocating what I believed to be good and I shall not begin now." In early 1918, Congress provided that railroads would revert to private ownership at the end of the war, but Bryan thought the matter not finally decided. In mid-1919, as Congress considered a bill to return railroads to private ownership, he presented his long-standing proposal for joint federal-state ownership. Despite some support for the "Plumb Plan," an alternative version of federal ownership, Congress voted to return the railways to private ownership.

As the war ended, Bryan issued his program for return to a peacetime economy. When Bryan listed fourteen points, few could fail to note the resemblance to Wilson's Fourteen Points for ending the war. Bryan's list included state and federal ownership of railroads and of telegraph and telephone systems, federal ownership of the merchant marine, protection of the public against profiteers, initiative and referendum at every level of government, reduction of government spending, tax relief for "those least able to bear the burden," and a national nonpartisan bulletin to inform the public of government actions. He considered such a bulletin especially important, perhaps because of the abuse often heaped upon him by the press. He had concluded that the media reflected conservative and Republican views, and that it distorted the views of progressives and Democrats. A nonpartisan bulletin would present news without the distortions that Bryan believed inevitable so long as the press remained controlled by private capital.

Bryan's fourteen-point program for post-war economic policy indicated his continuing interest in domestic reform. He also maintained his strong commitment to building a durable peace. He took an active part in the public discussion of the treaty ending the war; when Wilson began selecting members for the American delegation to the peace conference, Bryan made clear his availability. Fearing Bryan's propensity for utopian schemes, Wilson passed him over. The rejection deeply disappointed Bryan, but he praised Wilson's decision to attend the peace conference, and he endorsed Wilson's espousal of a league of nations.

Bryan's support for a league marked a change. In a widely reported exchange with former President Taft in 1917, Bryan had argued against the creation of a League to Enforce the Peace. He especially disliked the idea of an international organization empowered to use force in carrying out its decisions; such a provision, he feared, might drag the United States into future wars without the consent of its people, thus rendering the proposed league "a menace instead of a blessing." By early 1919, he still felt doubts about some details of the international organization being forged at Paris. Nonetheless, he found the League of Nations a distinct improvement over the balance of power as a means for maintaining international stability, and he labeled it "the greatest step towards peace in a thousand years." He could take special pride in Article XII, which established a process virtually identical to that of the Bryan conciliation treaties.

Bryan found a few faults in the treaty and in the League, but he had confidence that approval of the treaty would begin a process of eliminating war. The defects in the document, he thought, could best be remedied from inside the League. By promoting this view, Bryan supported Wilson against a body of senators, most of them Republicans, who sought either to reject the treaty or to modify it substantially. When it appeared that Senate opposition would defeat the treaty, Wilson refused compromise and undertook a national speaking tour to develop public support. Midway through his schedule, he collapsed, then suffered a stroke which left him partially paralyzed and unable to provide leadership when the treaty came to a vote.

When the Senate first voted on the treaty, it went down to defeat. Bryan reconciled his differences with Gilbert Hitchcock, now Democratic floor leader in the Senate, and they agreed that only compromise could save the League. Wilson remained adamant, expecting to make the treaty the central issue of the 1920 campaign. Bryan recalled his effort to make foreign policy a central issue in 1900 and remembered how that effort had failed. He broke publicly with the president, choosing the Jackson Day Dinner in January 1920 to announce to party leaders that they must compromise if they wished to salvage anything. Some saw Bryan's dramatic break with the president and his uncharacteristic embrace of compromise as an announcement of candidacy for a fourth presidential nomination, but Bryan gave no indication that he would seek the White House.

For a quarter of a century, whenever a presidential election rolled around, Bryan's supporters had urged him to run. The election of 1920 proved no exception. At sixty years of age, Bryan might have been the strongest candidate his party could field, but he refused to seek the nomination. As usual, he used *The Commoner* to promote a wide array of candidates. The Michigan state primary election included all potential candidates; despite Bryan's efforts to the contrary, his name remained on the ballot. He permitted no organized effort on his behalf, but still placed third, behind Herbert Hoover and William McAdoo. A poll conducted by the *Literary Digest* suggested that Democrats ranked him ahead of all potential Democratic candidates but three: Wilson, William Gibbs McAdoo, and Governor Edward Edwards of New Jersey. Edwards's campaign, Bryan thought, focused solely on opposition to prohibition.

Bryan plotted a political course for 1920 similar to his 1912 endeavors to secure a progressive platform and candidate. He feared that the convention might see an effort to weaken prohibition, and he believed he had to be present to defend the Eighteenth Amendment and its strong enforcement. He knew it would be difficult for the nation's leading advocate of prohibition to win election as a convention delegate from the beer-loving Democrats of Nebraska, but he also believed that it would be cowardly not to try. "It is better to be defeated," he wrote to his brother Charles, " than to confess defeat in advance." The Hitchcock organization had defeated Bryan when he ran for convention delegate in 1916; they tried to repeat the accomplishment in 1920. When the votes were counted, however, Bryan regained his place among the state's leading Democrats, taking third place among the candidates. He would go to the convention assured of his usual spot on the Resolutions Committee.

Among the Democratic delegates who gathered in San Francisco's Civic Auditorium, only a few could match the length of Bryan's experience—he had watched his first Democratic convention forty-four years before—and none could match the breadth of his acquaintance with rank-and-file members of the party. Unquestionably the best known figure in the convention, he must have expected to play his usual role and to write much of the platform. He entered the Resolutions Committee meetings hoping to commit the party to two major objectives: stringent enforcement of prohibition and modification of the Versailles Treaty. Both positions were contrary to the desires of the Wilson administration. Bryan also proposed a number of other matters for the platform, some drawn from the fourteen-point program he had issued earlier. The committee reflected the positions of the Wilson administration in almost every particular; Bryan lost on his two major efforts and on most of the lesser ones.

Undaunted, he took his proposals to the convention floor, speaking for forty-five minutes in a fashion that reminded one reporter of "an elder admonishing a newer generation." Democrats had to decide, he said, whether they wanted the nation to be a part of the League or not. Ratification of the Versailles Treaty without change was a noble ideal, but only compromise could save American participation in the League of Nations. Only by accepting that fact and getting on with ratification, he warned, could Democrats keep from their hands "the blood of people slaughtered." He demanded a firm posture on prohibition. "It is better," he told his party, "to have the gratitude of one soul saved from drink than the applause of a drunken world." At the close of the sermon, the convention erupted into twenty-three minutes of applause and demonstration. Throngs of delegates pressed forward to shake the hand of the teary-eyed Commoner. Nonetheless, his proposals went down to defeat. Someone compared him to an elderly rural uncle coming to visit in the city: "We give him the easiest chair, we treat him with affection; when he advises us about our affairs, we listen respectfully—but we go our own way."

The Democrats nominated their presidential candidate on the forty-fourth ballot, finally settling on James Cox of Ohio, for whom Bryan had little regard. Shortly after the Democrats adjourned, the Prohibition party held its convention in Lincoln, still the Bryans' legal residence, although they had spent little time there in recent years. Not surprisingly, the Prohibitionists sought to give their nomination to the nation's leading opponent of alcohol. Vacationing in Montana, Bryan rejected the honor and announced that he intended to remain a Democrat. Even so, he thought that neither his party's platform nor its candidates justified any effort beyond simply casting a ballot. For the first time since 1892, Bryan took no part in the presidential campaign, although he did travel two thousand miles, from Florida to Nebraska, to vote for Cox. The Democratic presidential ticket took slightly more than a third of the total vote, the party's worst showing up to that time in its history.

Bryan's dramatic cross-country journey to cast his ballot marked the last time he voted in Nebraska. In the spring of 1921, the Bryans announced a decision that had evolved slowly over the previous eight years. "Mrs. Bryan's health is such that it is necessary for us to live in the South," the announcement began, "and having tested Miami's climate for eight years, we have chosen that city for our permanent home." In fact, the Bryans had given little time to Nebraska since 1912. Bryan entertained political reasons for the move as well. In 1920, when he had been worried that he might fail to win election as a convention delegate from Nebraska, he had written to Charles that "it *may* be best to go as a delegate from some other state." Bryan's defeat for convention delegate in 1916, the likelihood of continued struggles with the Hitchcock faction, and the strongly anti-prohibition sentiments of most Nebraska Democratic voters all suggested that if he cherished any lingering hopes for elective office, living in Nebraska posed only problems. The official announcement of the move hinted at such possibilities: "By transferring my citizenship to Florida I shall increase my capacity for usefulness because, living there, I can take part in the politics of the State and share also in determining the State's position on national questions."

Almost immediately, Bryan received letters urging him to run for the Senate. The prospect of a Senate seat attracted Bryan. Torn between "my desire for private life and my appreciation of the opportunities that the Senate would offer for service," he acknowledged that "as a Senator I could help Florida and, to a still greater extent, aid the Democrats of the nation by getting our arguments before the voters." Nonetheless, he decided in early 1922 not to seek election because of his conviction that he could not "afford to be put in the light of a seeker after office or take the risk of defeat." The prospect of defeat formed the more serious impediment to running. "If, in a Democratic state, and after my experience in public life," Bryan wrote, "I was defeated for a nomination, my enemies throughout the country would make effective use of it, and it might, by discrediting me, impair my usefulness as a private in the ranks." Defeat, too, would "detract very much from the pleasure of living here."

Although W.J. chose not to seek office in 1922, Charles Bryan proved that Nebraska voters harbored no permanent antagonism for the family name. In 1922, he won the Democratic nomination for governor. Gilbert Hitchcock secured the Democratic nomination for the Senate, hoping to become the first Nebraskan to win a third term. W. J. Bryan and Hitchcock had patched up their differences during the struggle over ratification of the Treaty of Versailles, but the old animosity flared anew in 1920. Circumstances now dictated harmony. W.J. came to Nebraska to campaign for his brother and to give full support, as well, to Hitchcock. The Omaha publisher reciprocated, and the Nebraska Democratic Party experienced a brief period of unity. Charles secured the governor's office with nearly 55 percent of the total vote, but Hitchcock lost.

Taking office as governor meant that Charles could no longer manage *The Commoner*. W.J. had left all business aspects and most editorial decisions up to his brother from the beginning. He would trust no one else with editorial decisions, and he was unwilling to assume that burden himself. The paper's last issue appeared in April 1923, ending twenty-two years of publication. Charles had also managed W.J.'s Nebraska real estate investments and the bond portfolio that was kept in a Nebraska bank. These matters were also liquidated. It seemed to Grace that Bryan was working "with feverish haste to wind up his earthly affairs." Villa Serena was also sold; the stairway to its second floor posed a serious obstacle to Mary now that she spent most of her time in a wheelchair. They built a new, smaller home, all on one floor, and named it "Marymont."

Although Marymont was smaller than Villa Serena, Bryan still kept a saddle horse and a poultry yard. He proudly wrote to his grandchildren in early 1925 that he had made sixty cents selling a dozen eggs; he calculated that if he sold all the eggs, he would make "nearly a hundred dollars a year" in clear profit. Bryan needed no additional income from the sale of eggs. Sale of his real estate investments had netted a healthy profit, supplemented by a nationally syndicated weekly newspaper column on the Bible. Since 1919, he had maintained an association with a Washington law firm, acting as a lobbyist for Central American nations seeking loans. In the early 1920s he earned impressive lecture fees from a land promoter for touting the virtues of the Florida climate. Newspaper cartoonists, with only slight exaggeration, portrayed the Commoner entering the Millionaires' Club. Despite some reduction in his speaking schedules, he still taught his Sunday Bible class, speaking to several thousand in the open air.

Throughout the early 1920s, Bryan continued to promote the cause of economic reform. The administration of Warren G. Harding, he rapidly concluded, owed its soul to big business, and would provide no leadership in the struggle for economic justice. He advocated the cause of the farmer, victim of falling prices, and the worker, who saw court decisions erasing the labor legislation of the Wilson years. Bryan continued to push the idea of a national, nonpartisan bulletin on governmental affairs. In foreign policy, he urged that the United States cancel the wartime debts owed by the Allies in return for their promise to reduce armaments. When Harding died in 1923, the new president, Calvin Coolidge, inherited an administration rife with corruption. Revelations of dishonesty in several departments and agencies, involving members of the Cabinet in some instances, all seemed to promise a Democratic presidential victory in 1924.

As the 1924 presidential election approached, as usual, Bryan began to receive letters urging him to run; as usual, he turned them aside. He presented several progressive Democrats as likely candidates, including Charles Bryan. Bryan ran for delegate-at-large to the 1924 convention, traveling to every county in Florida to meet voters and ask their support both for himself and for dry, progressive candidates. William Gibbs McAdoo, a dry progressive, won the state's presidential primary; Bryan placed first among the candidates for delegate-at-large. He garnered nearly twice as many votes as any other candidate, a hopeful portent for the 1926 senatorial primary.

The 1924 convention met in New York City, home turf for a leading candidate, New York governor Alfred E. Smith. A Catholic of Irish parentage, Smith had forged a moderately progressive record on economic issues, but his criticism of prohibition guaranteed that Bryan would find him unacceptable. Oscar Underwood of Alabama also opposed prohibition and held the most economic conservative views of all the major contenders for the nomination. McAdoo was the third leading candidate. Over all discussions of the nomination, however, hung the specter of the Ku Klux Klan.

Originally formed following the Civil War to intimidate former slaves, the Klan had been revived in 1915, appealing to hatred of Catholics, Jews, blacks, Asians, and immigrants. Rapid growth began in 1920, as the Klan claimed to be leading a campaign against bootleggers, gamblers, brothel-keepers, wife beaters, and others who flaunted the Protestant moral code. Burning crosses and white-robed Klansmen soon became common sights. By 1924, the Klan claimed more than two million members nationwide. The hooded order mobilized its forces in politics from the beginning, helping to elect a few United States Senators and governors and scores of local officials throughout the South, Middle West, and Far West.

Both Underwood and Smith announced their opposition to the Klan, but McAdoo kept silent. No friend of the Klan, McAdoo nonetheless knew that some of his delegates supported it. The Klan gave McAdoo lukewarm support, opposed Smith because of his Catholic faith, and rejected Underwood because of his antagonism toward prohibition and the Klan. Early in the convention, Smith and Underwood supporters agreed to emphasize the Klan as a means of defeating McAdoo, and Smith supporters in the convention galleries lost no opportunity to yell "Ku, Ku, McAdoo."

Bryan arrived in New York pledged to McAdoo and prepared, as always, to do battle for his principles. As Florida's representative on the Resolutions Committee, Bryan presented a list of twelve platform planks he hoped to hammer in place. Eight proved acceptable to the committee, including limits on campaign contributions, enforcement of the constitution and all laws (including prohibition only implicitly), international agreements on disarmament and national referenda before any declaration of war, a national referendum on the League of Nations, and his usual declaration "that private monopoly is indefensible and intolerable."

Other platform provisions echoed those from the years from 1896 through 1912, when Bryan had been the major force in preparing the statements of party position. Bryan proposed a statement in defense of freedom of religion, but he sought to avoid condemning the Klan by name. The resolutions committee met for three days, laboring all night after the third day. They achieved no consensus on the Klan issue and adjourned after agreeing to submit majority and minority reports.

The platform debate began soon after the committee's adjournment. Just as in 1896, Bryan addressed the convention by defending the majority report. Just as in 1896, he spoke last. Just as in 1896, the early speeches were long, the crowd restless and demonstrative. Just as in 1896, Bryan came forward with a buoyant step. But the fresh face of the thirty-six year old had become gaunt and lined, the full head of dark hair had given way to baldness and a gray fringe hanging untidily over his collar. The great organ-like voice still filled the vast hall, but his baggy trousers, palm fan, and string tie seemed quaint and old-fashioned. The galleries booed and jeered. "The Ku Klux Klan," he lectured the minority report supporters, "does not deserve the advertisement that you give it." He pointed to the parts of the platform defending freedom of religion and condemning "any effort to arouse religious or racial dissension." He upheld the platform as "the best Democratic platform that was ever written," and argued that the Klan issue only diverted attention from the real issues: the distress of agriculture, the spread of monopoly, the needs of "war-worn" Europe. "Anybody can fight the Ku Klux Klan," he proclaimed, "but only the Democratic party can stand between the common people and their despoilers." Condemning the Klan by name would disrupt the party at a time when it was otherwise more united than ever before. "Christians," Bryan adjured, "stop fighting."

Bryan considered his speech an appeal for unity on economic issues and an effort to moderate ethno-religious conflict, and he soon wrote: "I do not know of any greater service I have rendered to the party" than his defense of the platform. Others, however, condemned the effort as an apostrophe to expediency or even a defense of bigotry. Voting on the platform began when Bryan closed his speech. The majority report passed by the tiny margin of 4.3 votes. Although the platform did not condemn the Klan by name, the bloodletting of the platform struggle had gone far to destroy the unity for which Bryan had so earnestly hoped.

The remarkably even balance between the two sides on the Klan issue pointed to the difficulty any candidate would have in achieving the two-thirds necessary to win nomination. Balloting quickly reached deadlock between Smith and McAdoo. Ballot followed ballot, day followed day, but the stalemate remained. After the thirty-seventh ballot, on the third day of balloting, Bryan asked to address the convention to explain his vote. Again he began amidst taunts from the galleries. Because of the deadlock, he said, he wanted to suggest some other candidates who might prove acceptable; he listed several, both Southerners and Northerners, including his brother Charles. "This is probably the last Convention of my party in which I shall be a delegate," he announced, only to be interrupted by applause from the Smith forces. He drew laughter and cheers when he promptly added "Don't applaud; I may change my mind," then went on to urge support for McAdoo. His speech generated telegrams from McAdoo delegates adjuring them to stand fast.

Both Smith and McAdoo held fast, and the balloting continued, day after hot, weary day, as some delegates began to wonder how they would pay their hotel bills. Will Rogers's quip, "I belong to no organized political party; I am a Democrat," never seemed more apt. The first ballot had been taken on June 30; on July 9, on the 103rd ballot, the exhausted delegates finally gave the necessary two-thirds of their votes to John W. Davis of West Virginia, a former member of the Wilson administration whom Bryan had long since dismissed because of his ties to J. P. Morgan. Bryan felt despondent until told that Davis had agreed to take Charles Bryan as his vice-presidential candidate. The impossible convention had taken its final bizarre turn, teaming J. P. Morgan's lawyer with W. J. Bryan's brother. As if Democratic chances of victory were not remote enough, Robert La Follette accepted the call of a Progressive third party. Bryan stumped through fifteen states, giving over a hundred speeches for Davis and his brother, but Coolidge won handily and the Davis-Bryan ticket got an even smaller portion of the vote than the Democrats had managed in 1920.

Bryan waited until early December to deliver himself of his analysis, but when he did he couched it in phrases from 1896: "The only hope of national success for the Democratic Party lies in a union between the producers of the South and West against the predatory corporations that dominate the politics of the Northeast. We cannot possibly get between the Republican Party and Wall Street. . . . The Democratic Party must be progressive if it is to be an important factor in national politics. The reactionary element of the country is not large enough to need two political parties to represent it—the Republican Party is sufficient." As 1924 turned into the new year, Bryan began to give serious attention to seeking the Florida seat in the United States Senate, which would come up for election in 1926.

While Bryan's commitment to economic reform and his interest in electoral politics remained as strong as ever, he acknowledged in early 1923: "My power in politics is not what it used to be." "While my power in politics has waned," he added, "I think it has increased in religious matters." His interest in religious subjects had deepened, he said, because "the brute theory has paralyzed the influence of many of our preachers and undermined the faith of many of our young people in college." By the "brute theory," Bryan meant evolution.

In the "Prince of Peace" speech, first given in 1904 and repeated and refined many times thereafter, Bryan had recounted his own doubts upon encountering differing theories on the creation of the universe. All such accounts left vital questions unanswered, he thought. He concluded that the account of creation in Genesis provided all the answers necessary. "You may trace your ancestry back to the monkey if you find pleasure or pride in doing so," he said, but added, "you shall not connect me with your family tree without more evidence than has yet been produced." He considered evolution to be dangerous, because people might "lose the consciousness of God's presence in our daily life." He objected as well to the concept of the survival of the fittest, "the merciless law by which the strong crowd out and kill off the weak," referring to it as "the law of hate." For Bryan, Christian love was the law by which the human race had progressed and developed.

At the end of the war, Bryan began to devote increasing attention to evolution and to efforts at bringing Christianity back to its "fundamentals." He explained his increased attention to evolution in part by citing a study by James H. Leuba, *Belief in God and Immortality*. Leuba appears again and again in Bryan's correspondence and speeches as the source for the statement that "half the prominent scientists of the United States do not believe in a personal God or a personal immortality." Such people, Bryan thought, became "mind-worshippers." Evolution, he argued, "discredits things that are supernatural and encourages the worship of the intellect." Bryan took even more seriously Leuba's discovery of a decline in religious commitment among college students; he attributed this loss of faith to their professors. "What shall it profit a man," he asked, "if he shall gain all the learning of the schools and lose his faith in God?"

Another factor in Bryan's increasing antagonism toward evolution derived from his conviction that it had laid "the foundation for the bloodiest war in history." Evolution, he thought, had produced Friedrich Nietzsche's writings, in which Bryan discerned "a defense, made in advance, of all the cruelties and atrocities practiced by the militarists of Germany." By 1925, Bryan had come to blame evolution, not only for the loss of faith among Christians and for the horrors of the war, but also for "the gigantic struggle that is now shaking society throughout the world." "Survival of the fittest," he proclaimed, was driving both capitalist and laborer "into a life-and-death struggle from which sympathy and the spirit of brotherhood are eliminated. It is transforming the industrial world into a slaughter-house."

Bryan also identified evolution as "the root cause of the dissension in both Church and school," two of the social institutions most central to the small-town and rural society from whence he came and in which he found his most devoted supporters, and he began to attempt a restoration of social harmony by purging evolution from both places. In doing so, he had to confront "Modernism," an attitude among many church leaders that science and the church need not stand in conflict but might find common ground; some Modernists suggested that the Scriptures allowed for the possibility that God worked through evolution. "Theistic evolution," Bryan proclaimed derisively, "is an anesthetic; it deadens the pain while the Christian's religion is being removed." Bryan's God did not work through evolution, but through miracles; his God was not a mere First Cause, but a continuing presence. The Modernists' "far-away God does not invite prayer," he complained, "or give comforting assurance of His presence." "There is no place in evolution," he added, "for the penitent soul; it knows no such transformation as being born again or having sins forgiven." Evolution, he contended, "robs a man's conscience of its compelling force."

Bryan's crusade against evolution put him in conflict, not only with the Modernists within most major Protestant denominations, but also with nearly all the nation's scientists.

The Commoner attacked them as readily as he did the Modernists. In attacking scientists, he tried to make clear that he did not attack science. During the 1920s, the nation had embraced science as never before. Newspapers carried columns dealing with new discoveries; the phrase "Science teaches us" became a certain means of ending an argument. Bryan sought to separate the scientists who promulgated evolution from science itself, but revealed only his own intellectual shallowness. "Religion has no quarrel with science," he said, because "nothing . . . can be scientific that is not true. All truth is of God, whether found in the book of nature or in the Book of Books." Evolution, he claimed, was only an hypothesis, a "guess." He often used "evolution" and "Darwinism" interchangeably, and pointed to Charles Darwin as the chief source of the problem. Having identified Darwin with evolution, he then knocked down his straw man by pointing out inconsistencies in Darwin's work or by indicating that subsequent scientists had discounted some parts of his analysis. Frequently, however, Bryan fell back on euphonious metaphors to argue that some questions were less relevant than others: "It is better to trust in the Rock of Ages than to know the age of rocks; it is better for one to know that he is close to the Heavenly Father, than to know how far the stars in the heavens are apart."

Bryan conducted his crusade against evolution, mind-worshipping scientists, and Modernists on three major battlefields, all of them familiar terrain. First, he attacked them on the lecture circuit, in his famous outdoor Sunday school, and through his weekly newspaper column. Second, he engaged them in the business meetings of the Presbyterian Church. He had long served as a lay delegate to various Presbyterian bodies and, in the early 1920s, used those occasions to embarrass the Modernists. In 1923, he sought election as moderator of the General Assembly, the highest elected national official of his church. Although he narrowly failed of election, he managed to secure passage of resolutions, much as he would have done on the floor of a Democratic convention. Third, he invoked his political contacts in state legislatures to try to secure legislation to restrict the teaching of evolution as anything but hypothesis. A number of states saw the introduction of bills, but Tennessee became the first state to prohibit the teaching of evolution altogether, a position more extreme than Bryan advocated.

The governor of Tennessee signed the anti-evolution measure on March 21, 1925. Within two weeks the American Civil Liberties Union (ACLU) condemned the law as a violation of academic freedom and announced that it would provide counsel to a Tennessee teacher willing to test the constitutionality of the law. By April 5, several leading citizens of Dayton convinced John Scopes to stand as defendant. Once the ACLU agreed to support the defense, Scopes was arrested and charged. The attorneys for the prosecution and the Christian Fundamentals Association both asked Bryan to join in defense of the Tennesse law; he agreed. The defense proved able to attract co-counsel nearly as renowned: Clarence Darrow, the most famous trial lawyer in the nation; Dudley Field Malone, who had served as an Undersecretary of State when Bryan had been Secretary; and Arthur Garfield Hays, attorney for the ACLU.

Bryan thought the case would be a valuable test for the law. "I don't think we should insist on more [than] the minimum fine," he wrote to the local prosecutor, "and I will let defendant have the money to pay it if he needs it." As he analyzed the situation in late May, "it is the *easiest* case to explain I have ever found." He was uncertain that evolution would enter the case at all, although he hoped to have several prominent ministers and scientists to testify against evolution. He felt that the "real issue" was "the *right* of the *people* speaking through the legislature, to control the schools which they *create* and *support.*" Bryan urged his son, a lawyer, to come to Dayton to take part. "This trial will become one of the greatest trials in history," he wrote, and William, Jr., finally agreed to take part.

The Bryans arrived in Dayton on July 7 and were guests of honor at a banquet that evening. There they met Scopes, who had grown up in Salem, Illinois, Bryan's birthplace. The little town of Dayton, nestled in a valley in the midst of the hill country of eastern Tennessee, with a population of some 1,800, must have seemed a slight variation on patterns Bryan and Scopes had known in Salem. Nearly everyone knew everyone else, most businesses occupied one- and two-story brick buildings along a few blocks of the main street, and maple trees surrounded the three-story brick court-house in the center of town.

The trial brought to Dayton a flood of outsiders—150 reporters, movie cameramen, and a throng of "medicine men, traveling evangelists, and screwballs," as Scopes put it. Revival preachers set up tents on the outskirts of town to hold prayer meetings and to seek converts. A Chicago radio station sent personnel to broadcast the trial nationwide. By the 1920s, the development of radio and changes in the nature of newspapers and magazines had produced what one close observer called "the ballyhoo years," during which the media wooed the public with one spectacular after another. The high drama of the Scopes trial, pitting against each other some of the best known personalities of the day on one of the most controversial subjects, promised greater ballyhoo than the treasures of King Tut's tomb or the bat-ting averages of Rogers Hornsby.

The trial began on Friday, July 10. The courtroom was packed, the temperature hot. Mary described the first week of the trial as "a great mixture of waving fans, perspiring men, and angry lawyers." When the Bryans entered the courtroom, Mary in her wheelchair, W.J. received a loud ovation in recognition of the twenty-ninth anniversary of his "Cross of Gold" speech. Darrow had sat with his law partner, John Peter Altgeld, in the 1896 convention and had cheered

Bryan's oration. Darrow and Bryan chatted for a time, then set the sartorial tone for the proceedings by removing their coats and facing the judge in shirt-sleeves. Counsel completed examination of potential jurors that day; the twelve jury members included eleven church members: six Baptists, four Methodists, and one Disciple of Christ. Over the weekend, Bryan preached both in the Methodist church and from the courthouse lawn. Several prominent Dayton citizens announced plans to create a Fundamentalist university with Bryan as president.

The following Monday, the defense moved to quash Scopes's indictment on the grounds that the law was unconstitutional. The judge heard arguments from both sides, considered the motion, and ruled against it on Wednesday morning, as the defense entered objections into the record. Both sides made opening statements, the prosecution represented by A. T. Stewart, the state's attorney for that judicial circuit, and the defense by Malone, who cited Bryan's description of the views of Thomas Jefferson: "to attempt to compel people to accept a religious doctrine by act of law was to make not Christians but hypocrites." The prosecution presented four witnesses who established that Scopes had taught science and biology, that he had presented the basic concepts of evolution, and that the state-approved textbook included brief explanations of evolution and of Darwin's role in its development. The defense did not deny that Scopes had taught evolution but argued instead that teaching evolution did not necessarily involve denying the divine creation of man. On Thursday morning, the judge heard defense arguments regarding the need for expert testimony on evolution and the Bible. Bryan presented a long oration in response.

The Commoner trembled when he stood to speak, revealing the impact of age, strain, and heat. Clad in dark baggy trousers, a white shirt, and a black bow tie, he recycled some metaphors and efforts at humor from previous writings on evolution, managing to garble its meaning. Despite gaffes which showed that Bryan had only the vaguest notions of what he was opposing, most of the address found him on familiar ground. He invoked the specter of Nietzsche and adduced his stock arguments that Darwin had been contradicted by more recent scientists. (The defense responded that such arguments supported their request to introduce expert testimony in order to establish exactly what evolution meant.) Scopes found himself "not listening to what he was saying, but to how he was saying it, . . . letting his oratorical talents hypnotize me. The longer he talked (a little more than a hour), the more complete was the control he had over the crowd."

The audience hung on Bryan's words and Scopes thought the faces in the crowd "showed reverence and worship." The audience erupted into a long ovation at Bryan's conclusion. Malone then presented the closing arguments for the defense, rising to a level of drama that forecast his later career as a character actor in Hollywood. His argument for calling expert witnesses was so eloquent that Scopes thought the once-hostile crowd was "eating out of his hand and had, for the time being, forgotten Bryan." When the bedlam of applause subsided, Stewart made a few anticlimactic comments, and the court stood in recess for the day. Bryan waited until the throngs had left, then turned to Malone and complimented him. "Dudley," he said, "that was the greatest speech I ever heard." Bryan knew his oratory had taken second place.

On Friday morning, the judge denied the defense request for presentation of expert witnesses but decided to permit the defense to insert written versions of that testimony into the record. The court then stood in recess until Monday morning to allow the defense to prepare its written statements. Over the weekend, W.J., Mary, and William did some sightseeing, and W.J. preached a open-air sermon in a small town twenty miles from Dayton.

On Monday afternoon, the court moved outside because of fear that the courtroom floor might not bear the weight of the crowd much longer. The trial seemed close to an end. Once reassembled on the courthouse lawn, with the judge and the attorneys seated on a wooden platform, the audience on the grass, the defense startled nearly everyone by calling Bryan as a witness on the Bible. Darrow had been planning this move all weekend as a means of introducing evidence regarding the logical complexities of requiring that classroom instruction agree with the Bible. Stewart objected strenuously, but Bryan seemed eager to cross verbal swords with Darrow. He took the witness chair, and for the next two hours Darrow fenced with him on the Bible.

The sixty-eight year old Darrow, self-proclaimed agnostic, long-time champion of organized labor and the underdog, set out to reveal the intellectual shallowness he discerned in his erstwhile political ally. Bryan entered the contest with confidence, intending to rout the hosts of error arrayed against him. Darrow asked Bryan about the great fish that swallowed Jonah and about Joshua's commanding the sun to stand still. In both instances, Bryan insisted that the Biblical account was true, that God could perform any miracle He chose, and that a Christian ought to accept the Biblical account as written. He departed from the actual words of the Scriptures, however, to indicate that Joshua must have halted the earth from revolving, rather than stopping the sun in the sky, for a literal reading of the passage would have required believing that the sun revolved around the earth. He also made clear that he did not understand the law of gravitation.

As Darrow became more insulting and abusive toward Bryan, Stewart again tried to stop the proceedings, only to be denied by the judge. Bryan indicated that he accepted the Biblical view that life on earth, except fish and those aboard Noah's ark, had perished in a flood in 2348 B.C. He refused

to admit that any civilization could be traced, uninterrupt-
edly, to an earlier date. Darrow professed surprise at so
literal an interpretation of the Bible and suggested ample
evidence of the uninterrupted history of several civilizations
older than that date. "Do you know of a single scientific man
on the face of the earth that believes any such thing as you
stated, about the antiquity of man?" Bryan replied, "I don't
think I have even asked one the direct question." Darrow
asked if Bryan had ever investigated "to find out how long
man has been on the earth?" Bryan responded that "I have
never found it necessary."

Darrow asked Bryan about the age of Chinese and Egyp-
tian civilizations, but Bryan demurred, stating only that
"they would not run back beyond the creation, according to
the Bible, six thousand years." Again and again, as Darrow
touched the fields of history, comparative religion, anthro-
pology, archaeology, linguistics, and geology, he found that
the Commoner could only profess lack of interest or point to
the Bible as the only evidence of which he was aware. For
the previous five years, Bryan had been the nation's leading
opponent of any criticism of the Bible. He now stood revealed as knowing little or nothing about those of whom he
had been so critical. One more great surprise was to come.
Darrow asked, "Do you think the earth was made in six
days?" Bryan replied, "Not six days of twenty-four hours."
The gasp of the startled Fundamentalists must have been
loud enough to carry over the national radio hookup. Their
champion not only admitted that the Bible stood subject to
interpretation, but added that it was not important whether
God made the earth in six days or in "six years or in six
million years or in six hundred million years."

The head of the prosecution team intervened, asking the
purpose of the examination. Bryan responded that Darrow's
"purpose is to cast ridicule on everybody who believes in the
Bible." Darrow, however, insisted that the purpose of the
defense was "preventing bigots and ignoramuses from con-

trolling the education of the United States." After further exchanges on the origin of humankind, Bryan again accused Darrow of having no other purpose than "to slur at the Bible." Darrow angrily denied the accusation and the two sexagenarians stood shaking their fists at each other as the judge recessed until morning.

On Tuesday morning, the court moved back indoors, but with access tightly controlled. The judge ordered the previous day's testimony expunged from the record, then charged the jury. Bryan had no opportunity to cross-examine Darrow, as he had hoped, nor was he able to deliver the closing speech he had been crafting for months. The jury absented itself for a few minutes, then returned with their verdict of guilty. The judge imposed the minimum fine, notices of appeal were entered by the defense, and everyone made a final speech expressing gratitude to the court, the community, and others.

Scopes's conviction, and the later action of the state supreme court in overturning it on a technicality, were less important in the short run than the events of Monday afternoon, when the best-known trial lawyer of the day had humiliated the most famous orator of the era. Each titan had grown up in a small town in the Middle West, each embodied the nineteenth century's fascination with the spoken word. Each had entered politics in the turbulent 1890s, each had long fought for the dignity of labor and the rights of the common people. Each held confidence in his principles so strong as to verge on arrogance. But when the iconoclasm of the Chicago lawyer met the piety of the Miami Sunday school teacher, the clash pitted science against religion, urban sophistication against rural innocence, academic freedom against anti-intellectualism. Like an old timber wolf clamping his jaws upon an ancient stag, Darrow showed neither mercy nor remorse. "Bryan was broken," one reporter wrote. "Darrow never spared him. It was masterful, but it was pitiful."

William Jennings Bryan preaching from the pulpit of the Dayton, Tennessee, Methodist Church, during the Scopes trial in 1925. (UPI/Bettman Archive)

I X

Evaluating a Crusader

AFTER THE SCOPES trial sputtered to its anticlimactic conclusion, the Bryans stayed in Dayton for a few days to tie up a number of loose ends. W.J. spent two days polishing the speech he had hoped to present as the prosecution's concluding argument, then traveled to Chattanooga to arrange for publication of the revised oration. He made a few speeches before returning to Dayton early on Sunday, July 26. After he looked over his mail and attended morning church services, he and Mary ate their noon meal. He made a few telephone calls, then laid down for an afternoon nap. He died in his sleep.

President Calvin Coolidge, Chief Justice William Howard Taft, the presidents of El Salvador and Peru, the legislature of the Philippines, the president of the American Federation of Labor, and the commander of the Salvation Army joined thousands of Bryan's long-time friends, political associates, and admirers in expressing condolences to Mary as she prepared for the funeral and burial. The mayor of Dayton proclaimed a day of mourning; the Klan burned crosses in memory of the nation's leading defender of evangelical Protestant values. Bryan's family chose Washington for the site of the funeral. The train which carried the Commoner to the capital for the last time provoked a massive outpouring of the faithful, who lined the tracks along the way as they had first done in 1896. Hundreds attended the funeral. Additional hundreds were turned away for lack of room. Radio carried the services nationwide. As Bryan had requested, burial took place in Arlington Cemetery.

Senator Henry Fountain Ashurst of Arizona told the press that Bryan's "superlative oratory, his frame of oak, and his apostolic zeal brought the income tax, woman suffrage, prohibition and direct election of senators." Gilbert Hitchcock called Bryan "the greatest moral force of his day." Vice-President Charles M. Dawes, who had known Bryan when they had offices in the same building in Lincoln, said that the Commoner "never did unworthy or mean things. He may have been mistaken at times as we all are, but he was trying always to do the right as he saw it." Victor Rosewater, who had tracked Bryan's career from the vantage point of the *Omaha Bee*, thought Bryan was "the most stubbornly wrong man I ever knew in politics, but he was perfectly sincere in his vagaries." H. L. Mencken, the acerbic editor of the *American Mercury*, denied Bryan even the virtue of sincerity, comparing him to P. T. Barnum. Mencken, who had produced scathing reports from Dayton, condemned the dead man as "a charlatan, a mountebank, a zany without sense or dignity"; he suggested that "Bryan lived too long, and descended too deeply into the mud, to be taken seriously hereafter by fully literate men, even of the kind who write schoolbooks."

Despite Mencken's malevolent prediction, Bryan was taken seriously after his death, and by others than those who write schoolbooks. Bryan Breakfasts and Bryan Dinners honored the memory of the Commoner until the advent of World War II. In 1933, Senator Elmer Thomas of Oklahoma, a long-time Bryanite, pushed through Congress a measure designed to counter depression by inflating the currency through silver coinage and other means. President Franklin D. Roosevelt took the nation off the gold standard the next day; Edgar Howard, a member of Congress who had served Bryan as secretary during the Commoner's first congressional term, praised Roosevelt because "the heavy cross of gold has been lifted from the backs of American citizens." In 1934, on Bryan's birthday, the House of Representatives passed a measure designed to reduce agricultural surpluses and simultaneously to increase the nation's silver supply. That same year, President Roosevelt spoke at the dedication of a Bryan statue in Washington. The Commoner's admirers named in his honor a museum, a library, and a park in Salem, a college in Dayton, a Methodist church in Florida, and a hospital in Lincoln. They dedicated a statue and a bust in Lincoln, as well as two statues in Washington; the one Roosevelt dedicated was subsequently moved to Salem, the other stands in the Capitol. The Nebraska State Historical Society has administered Fairview as a museum since 1976. Bryan's life and career have provided the subject matter for nearly twenty books, several dozen articles, and more than fifty masters' theses and doctoral dissertations. The judgements of these authors, both professionally trained historians and others, have ranged nearly as widely as the opinions of Ashurst and Mencken.

Most recent accounts of Bryan's career have agreed that Bryan had his flaws—nearly all point to a lack of intellectual depth—but most also agree on Bryan's sincere commitment to the people, to economic opportunity, to peace, and to democracy. For Bryan, every policy proposal had to be tested in the crucible of principle, and only those that passed the test earned his support. The two sets of interlocking principles most central to his thinking had deep roots in his Salem childhood, in the teachings of his father and mother, in the political rhetoric of Jacksonian Democrats, and in the preachings of evangelical, perfectionist Protestantism. One set of principles was based upon concepts of political equality, the other derived from his Protestant religious beliefs.

Bryan's first set of principles emerged especially from his reading of Thomas Jefferson, whom he considered the founder of his party. Jefferson had written that all men were created equal; Bryan concluded that all voters were, or should be, as nearly equal as possible in fact. (He knew, of course, that voters were as unequal in political influence as in intelligence, virtue, or merit.) The principle of equality, in turn, had both political and economic corollaries for him. Politically, it meant that all white males—he eventually added women—stood equally qualified to vote and hold office. Thus, in the 1890s, he opposed the efforts of the APA to exclude Catholics from office, and in 1924 he opposed the efforts of Al Smith supporters to exclude Klansmen from the Democratic party. It also meant that personalities were far less important than issues and principles. If all men stood equal, then any competent man with the proper principles could be entrusted with the loftiest of responsibilities; "deserving Democrats" with proper recommendations attesting to character and competence could be named to high foreign service positions without qualms for the quality of representation. Expertise counted for less than a good heart and a principled outlook. Bryan quoted Jefferson with approval: "The principles of right and wrong are so easily understood as to require not the aid of many counsellors."

Beginning with the belief that all citizens were political equals, Bryan drew the Jacksonian conclusion that they should share as equally as possible in the process of governing themselves. The extension of popular participation in government decision-making—the direct primary, the direct election of United States Senators, the initiative and referendum, woman suffrage—all provided a greater role for ordinary citizens and therefore deserved support. Political equality, for Bryan, produced a belief in the unassailable right of the majority to govern. Again quoting Jefferson, he proclaimed "absolute acquiescence in the decision of the majority" to be "the vital principle of republics." He did not claim that the majority could do no wrong, only that "the people have a right to make their own mistakes." He criticized violations of majority rule and vigorously defended the right of the majority to make decisions—both decisions limiting the property rights of a privileged few and decisions dictating to schoolteachers how they should present biology.

The economic corollary of equality was that all deserved an equal chance at success. "Equal rights to all and special privileges to none," Bryan often proclaimed, was the only appropriate rule for "all departments of government." Bryan drew upon his Jacksonian heritage when he argued that abnormally large incomes usually grew out of governmental privileges and favors. While Bryan's analysis of the political economy began with Jacksonian assumptions, he also recognized that the years after the Civil War had witnessed the emergence of huge corporations that sometimes monopolized entire industries. As a good Jacksonian, he traced the origins of this economic power to governmental favoritism. But Jacksonian solutions of minimal government no longer had relevance once the monopolies existed; minimal government, in fact, only gave the monopolies free rein. In seeking a solution to the problems posed by monopoly, Bryan parted company with his Jacksonian forebears and embraced the Populists' prescriptions for the use of government to control these economic giants. He advocated government ownership of the railroads long before any other major political figure. He did so because of his belief that government should remove barriers to individual achievement, especially those posed by the concentration of economic power in private hands. "A private monopoly," he never tired of repeating, "is indefensible and intolerable." In the case of railroads, he saw public ownership as the only viable alternative to private monopoly.

For Bryan, belief in equality, majority rule, and the highest possible level of popular participation in decision-making all gained additional legitimacy from the close relationship of these concepts to a second set of principles derived from his religious beliefs. Bryan's faith included, as its central elements, the fatherhood of God, the atonement of Christ, and the brotherhood of man. (For Bryan and others of his day, the "brotherhood of man" unquestionably included women.) Bryan's belief that all men were brothers reinforced and became inseparable from his belief that all men were equal. His belief in the fatherhood of God had close ties to his belief in self-government; he cited Henry Clay when he pronounced that "it would be a reflection on the Almighty to say that He created people incapable of self-government." The same concept reinforced his belief in the need to restrain corporate power. "There is increasing necessity," he wrote, "for legislation which will protect the God-made man from injustice at the hands of the law-created person, known as a corporation." He defined morality as a set of rules made by God; people obeyed these rules because of their desire for immortality. This concept of morality also became intertwined with his views on economic policy: "The man-made corporation cannot be endowed with a soul," and therefore could experience no inner compulsion to follow moral rules. If a corporation "can avoid punishment here," Bryan concluded, "it need not worry about the hereafter."

Bryan's religious faith converged with his Jeffersonian political principles to buttress his belief in the people and his commitment to controlling the new economic behemoths of industrial America. Bryan's faith gave him a personal sense of confidence and courage. In his "Prince of Peace" speech, he emphasized that a Christian gained inner peace through prayer and through assurance of immortality. Inner peace produced courage. "Only the man of faith," he averred, "can be courageous." He might well have been speaking of his own political career when he added: "If every word spoken in behalf of truth has its influence and every deed done for right weighs in the final account, it is immaterial to the Christian whether his eyes behold victory or whether he dies in the midst of the conflict." For him, the most important goal was not winning but, as he told the 1904 convention, knowing that he had "kept the faith," that he had fought with courage for principle. Because he believed his principles were not only right but also eternal, he had confidence that they would eventually prevail. He saw himself as the instrument for the spreading of truth, and he counted his success more by converts to his cause than by offices he won.

Bryan's faith in the people, working through democratic processes, and his faith in God, provided him with principles against which to test virtually any proposed policy. He has been widely criticized for failing to ground himself more thoroughly in the writings of leading political and economic analysts of his day. Richard F. Pettigrew, United States Senator from South Dakota throughout the 1890s and a leader of the Silver Republicans, thought that Bryan's library "contained almost no books whatever of value to a man fitting himself to be President of the United States or even a member of a State Legislature." Others have echoed Pettigrew's criticism. After leaving Congress in 1895, Bryan read mostly the Bible, Jefferson, the classics, and the popular press, but only occasionally did he conduct a detailed investigation of an issue. His constant traveling, speech-making, and column-writing left him little time for intense research or detailed analysis of his own; the day of elaborate research staffs for political figures had not yet arrived.

Edgar Lee Masters, who followed Bryan's career from 1896 onward, concluded that "by much talking and little thinking his mentality ran dry." The observation is a telling one. When Bryan left Congress and ceased to run for local elective office, he removed himself from the sharp give-and-take of congressional debate, as well as the debates of the campaign trail. He no longer needed to defend his statements against the criticism and refutation of a skilled political opponent in the same room. After 1895, Bryan typically found himself on a speaker's platform where few would challenge his statements, and he lapsed more and more into the role of oracle and sage, delivering himself of wisdom but never needing to respond to criticism or cross-examination. He came increasingly to evaluate issues primarily in terms of his Jeffersonian principles and religious beliefs, and in terms of the responses from lecture audiences and *Commoner* readers. From 1896 to the time of World War I, this approach usually put him in the vanguard of the nation's politics.

Bryan's political contributions fall into five areas: political structure and process, economic policy, foreign policy, social policy, and party leadership. In the area of political structure and process, there is no single reform for which Bryan could have claimed the largest part of the credit. He promoted proposals devised by others, and the passage of measures he advocated usually owed more to exertions by legislators, state or federal, than to his persistence. His role in support of a change was usually limited to speeches and newspaper columns; he seldom undertook the hard tasks of counting votes, lobbying doubters, and slowly building a majority. Nonetheless, during his career he attached himself to a wide variety of proposals for changing the political process, including many that gained acceptance. He advocated the direct election of United States Senators beginning with his first Congressional campaign in 1890 and continuing until final ratification of the Seventeenth Amendment. Though a late-comer to the cause of woman suffrage—where women's organizations had always played the major role—Bryan made speeches favoring changes in both state and federal constitutions. In his Chautauqua lectures, in political talks, in the columns of *The Commoner,* and in speeches to state legislatures, he advocated the initiative and referendum, and he played an important role in publicizing and popularizing those measures.

Other proposals of his for change in the political structure and process met rejection. He favored a one-term limitation on the presidency and wrote that provision into his party's platform; he backed down when Wilson sought a second term. After the treatment he received from the press in 1915, he continually advocated a government-issued, nonpartisan bulletin presenting political happenings and issues of the day, but he could not even persuade his own party to adopt that idea. As a variation on this measure, he advocated federal campaign assistance to guarantee candidates that their proposals would receive a public hearing regardless of the attitudes of the press but, in his own day, this proposal fared no better than the nonpartisan bulletin idea. He gave little time to two of the leading successful reforms in political structure during his own day, the movement for a permanent civil service and the elimination of partisan labels from political campaigns. Both ran contrary to his own deeply felt partisanship and his belief that a strong, principled party was the logical vehicle for achieving change.

While Bryan played primarily the role of publicist and popularizer for reforms in the political process, he could claim a more active role in the formation of economic policy. Much of his earliest political effort focused on tariff reform. As a member of Congress in the early 1890s, he played a central role in tariff revision efforts. Eventually, he came to categorize the tariff as the leading example of an "indirect tax," that is, a tax on consumption. Taxes on consumption, he thought, were concealed from the taxpayer; he argued that taxes should be direct and "easily scrutinized." Taking as his central principle that the taxpayer should "contribute to the support of his government in proportion to the benefits which he enjoys through the protection of his government," he argued that taxes on consumption varied "more nearly in proportion to men's needs than in proportion to their possessions," and compelled "the poor man to pay more than his share and the rich man less than his share." He advocated the graduated income tax on the floor of Congress in the 1890s, and he continued to promote it throughout his career, arguing that it distributed "the burdens of government" according to "the ability to contribute," compensated for the injustice of taxes on consumption, and discouraged large incomes.

Bryan considered taxation one of the "most far-reaching

subjects" government faced, and he put monetary and bank-ing policies into the same category. He posed two central guides to government monetary policy: "first, that the quan-tity of standard money shall keep pace with the population and business, and, second, that paper money shall be issued and controlled by the government." He believed that the expansion of the money supply in the late 1890s and early twentieth century, resulting from a substantial increase in the volume of gold, had established the quantity theory of money as beyond dispute. This, in turn, he saw as vindica-tion of his stand in favor of expanding the currency through silver. Throughout the early twentieth century, he continued to defend the quantity theory of money. While he did not originate that theory, he probably did more than any other public figure to popularize it, but he did not survive to see its final victory during the New Deal and after.

Bryan saw banking policy as closely related to monetary policy, and he made several important contributions to the nation's banking policy. He insisted that the issuance of money was a function of government, not of banks. Banking policy, he thought, should have as its object "to secure to the communities the banking accommodations which they need, with protection from the power that wealth gives to those who possess it." In his mind, "there is but one logical end to bank regulation, and that is the removal of every element of uncertainty so that money deposited in a bank can be drawn out at will." The Commoner applied this principle to the defense of bank inspection laws, reserve requirements, and limits on lending authority; in 1908, he prominently advo-cated an insurance fund for deposits, to be created by taxing banks. His supporters failed to write such a deposit insur-ance plan into the Federal Reserve Act in 1913, but a few hardy veterans of the 1908 campaign participated in 1933 when Congress created the Federal Deposit Insurance Cor-poration. Some of the changes in the Federal Reserve Act made by the Banking Act of 1935 followed pathways the

Commoner marked out in 1913, when he insisted that the Federal Reserve Board should be controlled by representatives of the public, appointed by the president, not by bankers.

While Bryan's direct effect on economic policy focused largely on taxation, monetary policy, and banking policy, he also exercised important indirect influences. During the late nineteenth century, the federal government had done little in the economy beyond stimulating economic development through such measures as tariff protection or land grants. During the early twentieth century, the federal government came increasingly to regulate economic activities. Regulation first emerged as a significant governmental activity during Theodore Roosevelt's administration, and was considerably extended under Woodrow Wilson. Bryan's campaign and his platform of 1900 had anticipated some of the measures Roosevelt later promoted, and his 1908 platform forecast some features of the Federal Trade Commission Act and the Clayton Anti-Trust Act, both passed in 1914.

Bryan's views of appropriate policy toward monopolistic concentrations of economic power usually owed more to his Populist allies than to the advocates of regulation, however. Typically he found himself closer to the attitudes of Robert La Follette and Louis Brandeis than to those of Theodore Roosevelt. In 1904, when federal and state governments were stepping hesitantly into the first serious regulation of railroads, Bryan boldly called for government ownership. In 1908, he stood for whatever legislation was necessary "to make it impossible for a private monopoly to exist in the United States." None of the measures of the Wilson administration went so far as Bryan's demand that no company be allowed to control "more than fifty per cent of the total amount of any product consumed in the United States." By constant opposition to monopoly and by calls for limitations on market shares and for government ownership, Bryan coaxed action from state and federal policy-makers; by such proposals, he also legitimized moderate reformers, such as Roosevelt, in the eyes of some business leaders who found their proposals more reasonable than Bryan's. In the "Cross of Gold" speech and in its innumerable repetitions, he dramatically contrasted economic policies based on creating prosperity from the top down with policies oriented toward creating a stable economic base, a theme his party would employ throughout the twentieth century.

Bryan hoped his impact on foreign policy would stand as high in significance as his contributions to economic policy. At the beginning of his political career, he gave little attention to foreign policy questions, mirroring perfectly the attitudes of the vast majority of Americans, including most office-holders. The Spanish-American War and the Treaty of Paris marked the inauguration of a new foreign policy by the McKinley administration, and Bryan soon moved to oppose the course of empire. He failed to make the 1900 election a referendum on imperialism, but his arguments nonetheless played an important role in solidifying public opinion against further acquisitions of colonies. His persistence in demanding independence for the Philippines finally helped to produce the Jones Act and its commitment to eventual independence although, as in the case of Bryan's views on monetary and banking policy, fulfillment of this promise came only in the 1930s with legislation setting a timetable for the transition in authority.

During the years after 1900, Bryan's foreign policy views continued to mature. Bryan's anti-imperialism had rested in major part on his politico-religious commitment to self-government. His later views incorporated an optimistic expectation widely shared among Americans of the early twentieth century that the human situation was steadily improving. For all Bryan's opposition to biological evolution, he accepted and even promoted the view that all human societies were evolving toward an ideal, and that the United States had moved the furthest in that direction. Bryan's concept of the ideal commonwealth rested upon self-government, the resolution of conflict through rational investigation, maximal opportunities for individual self-improvement, Christian service as the cornerstone of social relations, and a widely shared commitment to old-stock Protestant moral standards. His foreign policy views combined these attitudes with the traditional American commitment to remaining apart from world affairs. It produced both his conciliation treaties and his policy toward Latin America. While more reluctant than Wilson to intervene in the internal affairs of Caribbean nations, Bryan sometimes accepted intervention on the grounds that it would set the other nation more securely on the road to a higher level of development that would, in turn, render future interventions unnecessary.

The war that began in August 1914 profoundly affected Bryan at both personal and political levels. Like Wilson, he understood that the magnitude of the conflict made it impossible for the United States to ignore the events in Europe. His first priority was to prevent American belligerency, and he was willing to forgo traditional rights of neutrals in the accomplishment of that objective. His second objective was to restore peace in Europe, and he tried to maintain an even-handed attitude toward contending powers in hope of being able to serve as mediator. To the time of his resignation, he retained the hope that the United States might appeal to the rationality of the belligerents and to end the war through the investigatory processes he valued as the alternative to conflict. Such a role, clearly, would also have been the highest level of Christian service. Wilson placed a higher value on maintaining neutral rights, and in the end the belligerent powers proved unwilling to accept mediation.

Once war came, Bryan's immediate transformation to patriot obscured an important transformation from isolationist into internationalist. Bryan accepted the League of Nations, with or without modifications, as the best available instrument for forging a more rational, more humane world, and thereby he helped undercut somewhat the tide of isolationism that engulfed the nation at the end of the war. His conciliation treaties constitute his most lasting contribution to foreign policy. Several historians have suggested they would have brought Bryan a Nobel Peace Prize at any time other than 1914–1915. The conciliation concept itself became a part of the charters of both the League of Nations and the United Nations. Bryan's isolationist attitudes from the period 1914–1917 also found reflection in policy when Congress passed the Neutrality Acts of 1935, 1936, and 1937. Intended to avoid participation in another war in Europe, the acts prohibited loans to belligerents, prohibited American citizens from traveling on belligerent ships, and in other ways limited the neutral rights that Wilson and Lansing had so stoutly defended.

In the end, Bryan had more impact on foreign affairs as a critic of others' policies, rather than as a policy-maker in his own right. As secretary of state, he found himself unable to implement any but a few of the anti-imperialist tenets he wrote into Democratic platforms from 1900 through 1912. Wilson turned down his suggestion for a new Monroe Doctrine aimed at corporate intervention in western hemisphere governments. Bryan's devotion to conciliation produced thirty treaties, but they failed to prevent conflict. He was unsuccessful in his efforts to maintain American neutrality by restricting loans and travel, and Wilson rejected his proposals to seek an end to the conflict through mediation. A poll of diplomatic historians published in 1981 ranked him among the five worst secretaries of state, but that judgment seems too severe. Bryan served a strong-willed president who took a prominent role in foreign affairs and who preferred the advice of others to that of Bryan. To Bryan's credit, when he recognized the constraints within which he found himself, he extricated himself rather than mouthing phrases he did not believe, and he attempted to use his resignation to move policy in the direction he thought appropriate.

If Bryan's contributions to foreign policy reveal a strong missionary impulse, so do his attitudes regarding governmental social policy. Bryan believed that "each individual finds his greatest security in the intelligence and happiness of his fellows." He drew the corollary that every person should "exert himself to the utmost to improve conditions and to elevate the level upon which all stand." These views provided a rationale for government intervention in the economy to prevent oppression of the weak by the powerful; they provided as well a rationale for government intervention in social behavior, to prevent oppression, moral dissipation, and loss of faith. Bryan saw alcohol as a danger comparable to that posed by monopoly and he proposed similar remedies: purge of the offending element. Just as he would prohibit monopolies, so would he ban alcohol. Bryan devoted enormous energies to the prohibition cause, speaking widely and lobbying legislators at state and federal levels.

Bryan took a more tolerant position on religious matters than did many Americans of his day, certainly more tolerant than most of his fellow evangelicals. He worked closely with Catholics from his earliest days in Nebraska politics; his opposition to the anti-Catholicism of the American Protective Association provided a margin of victory by which he gained control of the state Democratic party in 1894. His lists of potential presidential candidates in 1912, 1920 , and 1924 carried the names of Catholics and Jews. (Nor did Bryan discriminate on the basis of region in his lists of potential candidates, proposing Southerners at a time when his party had not nominated a resident of the South since 1844.) Bryan's lists of potential candidates reflected his deeply felt belief in political equality and in the primacy of issues rather than personalities. So far as he was concerned, a dry, progressive Catholic would be acceptable for the presidency, but a wet, conservative Baptist would not. While his and Mary's personal friendships included Cath-

olics and Jews as well as Protestants, he showed little understanding of groups outside the Judeo-Christian tradition.
Bryan's treatment of Buddhism, Confucianism, Hinduism,
and Islam suggests a presumption that their adherents were
"heathen" and misguided.

Bryan tempered his views on race by a profound commitment to the principle of self-government. While he argued
strongly that people of color were fully capable of self-
government, he was always careful to distinguish between
the Philippines, Japan, Mexico, or India, on the one hand,
and the American South on the other. In cases of peoples
outside the United States, he considered that most of the
population stood roughly equal in political abilities. In the
American South, however, he considered the two races living there distinctly unequal in political competence. In
Bryan's analysis, whites had become "proficient" in government through the experience of "thousands of years." By
contrast, only "a few centuries" had passed "since the ances-
tors of the colored people of the South were brought from
Africa as slaves." Blacks, he thought, could not be expected
to show the same governmental abilities as the white race.
Although his relatively moderate views garnered him significant black support for his third presidential effort in
1908, he did nothing to oppose the segregation of the federal civil service during the Wilson administration. Like
most Americans of his day, he acquiesced in the legal disenfranchisement of black citizens in the South, and he accepted southern views that this protected good government.

Bryan considered blacks to be as capable of self-government as other people of color; he may have thought American blacks would eventually develop abilities for government
equal to those of whites. He considered education an important force for improving black political abilities, and he opposed reducing levels of funding for the black school systems
of the South. Until blacks demonstrated to him the level of
political ability which he felt characteristic of whites, he justi-

fied white supremacy policies in the South as producing benefits "not only [for] the advanced race but for the benefit of
the backward race also," because "the blacks have the advantage of living under laws that the white man makes for himself
as well as for the black man." The Commoner claimed that
southern blacks were denied only the right to form a political
majority, and he claimed that they received equal protection
of their other rights. To claim that blacks received equal protection of rights must have soothed the conflict between
Bryan's principles of equality and the attitudes of his southern supporters, but he must have had a difficult time ignoring the realities of discrimination and denial of rights everywhere in the South. Indeed, he could only have believed what
he said if he refused to look around himself when he and his
family lived in Texas, North Carolina, or Florida. On the
other hand, he undoubtedly spoke accurately when he
claimed that "there is not a state in the Union in which whites
would permit black supremacy," and thereby he lodged a
charge of hypocrisy against those Northerners, mostly Republicans, he said, who criticized the disenfranchisement of
blacks in the South. "White supremacy," Bryan concluded,
"promotes the highest welfare of both races."

While Bryan's attitudes deserve to be described as racist,
they differed little from those of most Democrats of his day.
In fact, the Commoner's views show more toleration than
might be anticipated in one whose parents were of southern
descent, and whose base of support within the Democratic
party included sizable portions of the South. On questions of
race, he did little to promote his views that blacks would
evolve to a status of political capability or to moderate unjust
features of policy in line with those views. Neither did he
support the extension of discriminatory laws. Such acquiescence in the dominant attitude within his party was unusual
for the Commoner. Usually he felt it incumbent to stake out
policy positions and to advocate them.

From 1890 on, Bryan played the role of party leader, first

in Nebraska, then on a national level from 1896 to his death. He ranks among the most significant leaders of the Democratic party from the time of its founding to the present. During the years from 1890 to 1925, only Grover Cleveland and Woodrow Wilson could challenge his preeminence. Of the two, Cleveland evoked that part of the spirit of Andrew Jackson which opposed the use of government, but he largely ignored elements in the Jacksonian heritage that condemned monopoly. The party of Cleveland could unite on the basis of opposition to the use of government: southern Democrats opposed federal intervention in their definition of racial matters, while some northern Democrats trained their sights on prohibition and others condemned protective tariffs. Wilson shared views close to those of Cleveland until late in his political evolution. When Wilson finally emerged as a progressive, the Democratic party had already undergone a transformation from a party hostile to the exercise of government to a party committed to use government "to make the masses prosperous," as Bryan put it. Bryan played the key role in that transformation, which revived the antimonopolism of Jackson but interred his belief in minimal government.

Bryan led the party during that transition, but his role was primarily that of popularizer rather than creator of the new definition of the role of government. Part of the new definition had been developed by Republicans who, from 1861 onward, had used government to stimulate economic development. The Populists moved beyond mere economic stimulation to advocate new uses of government to control—even to own and operate—the great concentrations of economic power which had emerged during the industrial development of the previous two decades. Bryan did not invent the idea of using government to control concentrations of power, but he saw the Populists as allies from their beginnings in 1890. He took some of their ideas and thrust them to the forefront of political debate by his oratorical prowess.

Bryan did not work alone in his efforts to move the Democratic party away from the conservatism of Cleveland, sharing leadership with Altgeld, Bland, Tillman, and many others who opposed that president's policies. He and others worked to maintain the party's new commitment to a positive concept of government, its commitment to restraining great concentrations of economic power, and its commitment to increasing the role of the citizen in the political process. Bryan's compelling voice and engaging smile won a personal following in 1896, which he could call upon in future years in support of his principles. By that dramatic campaign, he became the symbol of the transformation taking place within his party, and hence, within politics more generally. By spending the next twenty-nine years traveling about the nation, speaking to grass-roots leaders of his party, lecturing to throngs of citizens, sending out his views through his newspaper, *The Commoner,* and boldly battling in convention after convention, he built upon the following he had created in 1896 to carve out an unusual role in American politics. He spent little time in office—only four years in the House of Representatives and twenty-seven months as secretary of state. Nonetheless, the Commoner left a greater impression on public policy than at least ten of the fifteen presidents who held office during his lifetime.

The role Bryan defined for himself from 1896 to 1925 was that of a crusader, a fighter moved by deep and zealous commitment to a cause. He made the metaphor explicit in his famous speech before the Chicago convention in 1896, likening the commitment of the silver Democrats to "the zeal which inspired the crusaders who followed Peter the Hermit." "Clad in the armor of a righteous cause" (another metaphor from the same speech), Bryan fought tirelessly throughout his career for one issue after another. In Bryan's mind, righteousness required more than a passive avoidance of improper behavior. Humankind, in his view, stood capable of approaching perfection; his faith required him to do whatever in his power to remove the obstacles that prevented people from achieving their full, God-given potential. Once Bryan had decided that a cause was righteous, his faith obligated him to pursue that cause with a zeal and earnestness that set him apart from most other politicians, reformers and conservatives alike. Once committed, he held doggedly to a cause long after other politicians moved on to other concerns. Thus, he continued to fight for silver until 1906, ten years after its defeat; similarly, he continued to fight for Philippine independence for sixteen years after his initial defeat. He never admitted defeat, but sometimes found solace in partial victory.

Historians have observed that, in his crusades, Bryan tended to reduce complex issues to simple dichotomies, then to assign moral dimensions to the two sides. Once reduced to moral absolutes, compromise became impossible because any compromise required accepting some degree of immorality. In all fairness to Bryan, many issues he faced early in his career lent themselves easily to dichotomization: election of senators by the people versus election by state legislatures, the income tax versus no income tax, the gold standard versus a bimetallic standard, independence for the Philippines versus retention of the islands. In each of these instances, he was not alone in defining the issue as having only two sides, nor was he alone in attributing righteousness to one side. Further, although Bryan began with a principled position, he could accept various specific measures so long as they did not violate his principles. With respect to the tariff, for example, he argued that the tariff, as a tax, should be highest on luxuries and lowest on necessities. In the case of income tax, he preferred a progressive rate but accepted a flat rate as better than no income tax at all.

The middle of Bryan's career, from 1900 to 1910, reveals few instances where he reduced a complex issue to a simple one. His 1908 platform was one of the longest and most complicated up to that time. While he might have dramatically argued that private monopoly was intolerable, he posed a variety of solutions, including government ownership, licensing and regulation, and anti-trust actions. During the last fifteen years of his life, he again found a series of issues which proved susceptible to easy dichotomization: entry into war, prohibition, woman suffrage, the teaching of evolution as fact. So far as he was concerned, all these issues had but two sides. Most other politicians of the day shared that view. In a day when politicians think routinely of the thirty-second television commercial, it seems peculiar to criticize Bryan for oversimplifying issues, for his favorite campaign tactic was to present himself to as many people as possible, to speak to them for an hour or more, then to publish those speeches and distribute them as widely as possible.

Constantly in the public eye, Bryan exuded sincerity, honesty, geniality, and wholesomeness. Confident in his political and religious beliefs, he insisted always on the primacy of principles. He did not present issues with the detached and dispassionate approach of the intellectual. When an issue struck him as "paramount"—a favored adjective—he treated the cause with immediacy and passion. Such zeal typically gave an urgent moralism to his presentation of issues. His habit of clothing almost every issue in Biblical metaphors compounded the sense of moral earnestness.

Bryan was no intellectual. James Bryce, who was an intellectual, once wrote to a friend that Bryan struck him "as almost unable to *think* in the sense in which you and I use that word. Vague ideas floated through his mind but did not unite to form any system or crystallize into a definite practical proposition." Bryan may not have been an intellectual, but a survey of the occupants of the White House since World War II should establish that intellectuality is no more a requirement in our day than it was in Bryan's. The Commoner was certainly as intellectually capable as half of the men who have filled the presidency since the Civil War.

A reading of Bryan's speeches, even the most famous and

most often reworked, reveals vagueness in organization and ambiguity in analysis. The key to understanding Bryan is to approach him on his own terms rather than with the expectation of finding a carefully worked out analytical system. As an evangelical Protestant, his concepts of Christian duty and service and his belief in perfection led him to seek to rescue people from industrial oppression and from immorality. As a public figure, he found Christian love more compelling than logic. As a political leader, his constant contact with ordinary citizens did more to shape his policy positions than exhaustive research or formal analysis. As a public speaker, he employed oratorical metaphors that common citizens could understand, rather than formalistic structures or legalistic phraseology. As a political thinker, he felt a sincere, unshakeable confidence in the ability of the people to govern themselves. This confidence was reciprocated by a popular following with few parallels in American politics. Bryan's magnetic personality, his oratorical talents, and the force of his principles combined to produce unshakeable devotion among thousands.

A Note on the Sources

THE STUDENT OF William Jennings Bryan's life and career faces a huge volume of materials produced by him and by his wife, Mary Baird Bryan. There are three major collections of manuscript materials, including letters received by the Bryans, some copies of their outgoing correspondence, scrapbooks, copies of speeches, and the like. The largest is at the Library of Congress, but it includes little outgoing correspondence until quite late in Bryan's career. The collection at the Nebraska State Historical Society, Lincoln, includes scrapbooks and some letters and other materials. The collection at Occidental College, Los Angeles, donated by William Jennings Bryan, Jr., includes a good deal of interesting family correspondence, as well as a collection of Mary Bryan's speeches. The materials in the National Archives may be found in duplicate form with the Library of Congress materials. Some materials are also to be found in the Illinois State Historical Society. Bryan's letters appear in many other manuscript collections; a long list may be found in the bibliography to Louis W. Koenig, *Bryan: A Political Biography of William Jennings Bryan* (New York, 1971).

Bryan's published writings are numerous. Space permits listing only some of the most important for an understanding of his career and thought. Before his death, Bryan began work on *The Memoirs of William Jennings Bryan* (Philadelphia, 1925); Mary Baird Bryan completed the work with the assistance of professional writers. Many of the sections done by Bryan are variations on some of his speeches or other writings. *The Commoner,* a weekly from 1901 to 1913, then a monthly until 1923, includes nearly all of the speeches Bryan gave during the years the paper appeared (1901–1923). During the first seven years of *The Commoner,* the major speeches, editorials, and commentary were collected in annual volumes called *The Commoner Condensed*, published variously in New York, Lincoln, and Chicago. Many of Bryan's books were, in fact, compendiums of speeches, editorials, and columns strung together with a brief narrative. Among Bryan's most important political books are: *The First Battle: A Story of the Campaign of 1896* (Chicago, 1896); *Republic or Empire? The Philippine Question* (Chicago, 1899); *The Second Battle* (Chicago, 1900); and *A Tale of Two Conventions* (New York, 1912), which deals with the 1912 conventions. Large portions of the Democratic national platforms for 1896, 1900, 1904, 1908, and 1912 were written by Bryan, and those of 1900 and 1908 were almost solely his work; see Donald Bruce Johnson and Kirk H. Porter, comps., *National Party Platforms: 1840—1972* (Urbana, 1973). Nebraska Democratic platforms from 1888 through 1909 often included Bryan's ideas; see *Nebraska Party Platforms: 1858–1940* (Lincoln, 1940). For an account of Bryan's views on state government, see *The People's Law* (New York, 1914), a speech given to the Ohio constitutional convention in 1912. Regarding his ideas on international arbitration, see "The Forces That Make For Peace," World Peace Foundation Pamphlet Series (Boston, 1912). Bryan's actions in Nebraska politics are best followed in the major Nebraska newspapers, especially the *Omaha World-Herald,* the *Omaha Bee,* and the Lincoln *Nebraska State Journal.*

Accounts of Bryan's travels appeared in *Under Other Flags* (Lincoln, 1904) and *The Old World and Its Ways* (St.Louis, 1907). Books on religion include: *In His Image* (New York, 1922); *Famous Figures of the Old Testament* (New York, 1923); *Orthodox Christianity vs. Modernism* (New York, 1923); *Seven Questions in Dispute* (New York, 1924); *Christ and His Companions: Famous Figures of the New Testament* (New York, 1925); and *The Dawn of Humanity: The Menace of Darwinsim and the Bible and Its Enemies* (Chicago, 1925). For most of Bryan's major speeches up to 1911, see *Speeches of William Jennings Bryan,* 2 vols. (New York, 1911). His most popular Chautauqua talks were published as small books in New York in 1914; among the most important are: *The Prince of Peace, The Royal Art* (which deals largely with government), *The Message from Bethlehem* (mostly an exposition of his views on international relations), *The Value of an Ideal, The Price of a Soul,* and *Man.* Bryan had published in pamphlet form nearly every major speech he delivered, but I have not located a complete set of these pamphlets in any of the various Bryan collections. The most complete listing of Bryan's writings is to be found in the bibliographies to the three volumes of Paolo E. Coletta's *William Jennings Bryan* (Lincoln, 1964–1969). For a selection of Bryan's speeches and writings, with a very critical introduction, see Ray Ginger, ed., *William Jennings Bryan: Selections* (Indianapolis, 1967). Ginger portrayed Bryan as ignorant, foolish, and indifferent to facts. In a phrase almost worthy of Mencken, Ginger claimed that "the contents of [Bryan's] mind resembled cooked oatmeal." For a much more sympathetic collection with the material selected by Bryan's son, see Franklin Modisett, ed., *The Credo of the Commoner: William Jennings Bryan* (Los Angeles, 1968).

For the memoirs of those close to Bryan, see the sections by Mary Baird Bryan in the *Memoirs* (especially the selections from her journals) and similar sections by Mrs. Bryan in several other books, including *The First Battle;* Grace Dexter Bryan Hargreaves, "William Jennings Bryan: Biographical Notes, His Speeches, Letters and Other Writings" (unpublished manuscript, Bryan Manuscript Collection, Library of Congress); Arthur F. Mullen, *Western Democrat* (New York, 1940); George W. Norris, *Fighting Liberal* (New York, 1945) and "Bryan as a Political Leader," *Current History*, 22 (1925): 859–867; Charles McDaniel Rosser, *The Crusading Commoner* (Dallas, 1937); and Charles Willis Thompson, *Presidents I've Known and Two Near Presidents* (Indianapolis, 1929). Other memoirs of interest include: William G. McAdoo, *Crowded Years* (Boston, 1931); William Allen White, *Masks in a Pageant* (New York, 1939), and *Autobiography* (New York, 1946); John T. Scopes and James Presley, *Center of the Storm* (New York, 1967); Clarence Darrow, *The Story of My Life* (New York, 1932); Josephus Daniels, *The Wilson Era—Years of Peace, 1910–1917* (Chapel Hill, 1944); Charles G. Dawes, *A Journal of the McKinley Years* (Chicago, 1950); James Manahan, *Trials of a Lawyer* (St. Paul, 1933); Constantin Dumba, *Memoirs of a Diplomat* (Boston, 1932); David F. Houston, *Eight Years With Wilson's Cabinet*, 2 vols. (Garden City, 1924–1926); Willis J. Abbot, *Watching the World Go By* (Boston, 1933); and Robert Lansing, *The War Memoirs of Robert Lansing: Secretary of State* (Indianapolis, 1935).

Many biographies of Bryan were published at the time of his presidential campaigns. They include: C. M. Stevens, *Bryan and Sewall and The Great Issue of 1896* (New York, 1896); Richard L.

Metcalfe, *Life and Patriotic Services of Hon. William J. Bryan* (n.p., 1896); Harvey E. Newbranch, *William Jennings Bryan: A Concise But Complete Story of His Life and Services* (Lincoln, 1900); Richard L. Metcalfe and A. J. Munson, *Victorious Democracy* (n.p., 1900); Albert L. Gale and George W. Kline, *Bryan the Man* (St. Louis, 1908); and Richard L. Metcalfe, comp., *The Real Bryan* (Des Moines, 1908), the last a collection of speeches and writings. Some of these included a biographical sketch by Mary Baird Bryan.

Several biographies of Bryan appeared in the 1920s and early 1930s, including two by Wayne C. Williams, *William Jennings Bryan, A Study in Political Vindication* (New York, 1923) and *William Jennings Bryan* (New York, 1936). Williams admired Bryan deeply and his books take an almost totally sympathetic view of their subject. Genevieve Forbes Herrick and John Origen Herrick wrote *The Life of William Jennings Bryan* (Chicago, 1925) in the three weeks following Bryan's death; it is based on a quick survey of easily available materials and contains little of additional interest. J. C. Long's *Bryan: The Great Commoner* (New York, 1928) is better written but basically intended as a popular history; the same may be said of M. R. Werner's *Bryan* (New York, 1929). Long treats Bryan more sympathetically than does Werner. Not so *The Peerless Leader: William Jennings Bryan* (New York, 1929) by Paxton Hibben, with the manuscript completed by C. Hartley Grattan after Hibben's death; Hibben treated Bryan critically, often harshly, and also produced the first fully documented biography. Merle E. Curti, *Bryan and World Peace*, Smith College Studies in History, vol. 17 (1931), presented Bryan's tenure as secretary of state in a sympathetic fashion.

Richard Hofstadter, *The American Political Tradition* (New York, 1948), found Bryan lacking in both detachment and intellectuality, thought his religious views "childish" and his concept of democracy "inchoate," and considered him only "a provincial politician following a provincial populace in provincial prejudices." Most treatments of Bryan since then have taken a more sympathetic view. The years since 1960 have seen a proliferation of Bryan biographies, of which the most important by far is Paolo E. Coletta's three volumes (cited above), supplemented by some twenty articles presenting additional details and by *The Presidency of William Howard Taft* (Lawrence, 1973). His treatment seems destined, both by depth of research and the sheer bulk of the text, to stand as the definitive biography of the Commoner. Louis W. Koenig, a political scientist, produced *Bryan: A Political Biography of William Jennings Bryan* (New York, 1971), a work less than half the length of Coletta's work, but in one volume. It has a useful list of Bryan letters. Charles Morrow Wilson, *The Commoner: William Jennings Bryan* (Garden City, 1970), intended as a popular biography, is not documented, and is unreliable in places.

The years since 1960 have also seen several treatments of particular aspects of Bryan's career. Paul W. Glad, *The Trumpet Soundeth: William Jennings Bryan and His Democracy, 1896–1912* (Lincoln, 1960), started historians' reevaluation of Bryan's career and is a most useful treatment of cultural influences on the young Bryan. Lawrence W. Levine, *Defender of the Faith: William Jennings Bryan: The Last Decade, 1915–1925* (New York, 1965), took as its topic the other end of the Commoner's career from that studied by Glad. It provides balanced and informative coverage. Williard H. Smith, *The Social and Religious Thought of William Jennings Bryan* (Lawrence, 1975), brings together several essays by Smith which appeared previously in journals. David D. Anderson, *William Jennings Bryan* (Boston, 1981), is intended as a literary biography, focusing on Bryan as a writer. Kendrick A. Clements, *William Jennings Bryan: Missionary Isolationist* (Knoxville, 1982), examines Bryan's foreign policy views and contributions; Clements's views have influenced my treatment of Bryan's attitudes toward foreign policy. Paul Glad has also edited a collection of articles on Bryan: *William Jennings Bryan: A Profile* (New York, 1968). Another important interpretation of Bryan's contributions is to be found in J. Rogers Hollingsworth, *The Whirligig of Politics: The Democracy of Cleveland and Bryan* (Chicago, 1963).

For Bryan's childhood and youth, in addition to these sources, see the population schedules for the 1870 census (National Archives Microfilm Publications, microcopy no. 593; Washinton, 1965), the Salem *Advocate*, and *History of Marion and Clinton Counties, Illinois* (Philadelphia, 1881). For patterns of agriculture, see Paul W. Gates, *The Farmers' Age: Agriculture,1815–1860* (New York, 1960), and Fred A. Shannon, *The Farmer's Last Frontier: Agriculture, 1860—1897* (New York, 1945). For the Bryans' years in Jacksonville, see George R. Poage, "The College Career of William Jennings Bryan," *Mississippi Valley Historical Review*, 15 (1928): 165–182; and Don Harrison Doyle, *The Social Order of a Frontier Community: Jacksonville,*

Illinois, 1825–1870 (Urbana, 1978). For life in small Middle Western towns more generally, see Lewis Atherton, *Main Street on the Middle Border* (Bloomington, 1954). On Protestant evangelicalism, Timothy L. Smith, *Revivalism and Social Reform* (New York, 1957), is essential.

The best overview of political practices in the late nineteenth century is still that in James Bryce, *The American Commonwealth*, 2 vols., 2nd ed., rev. (London, 1891), especially chapters 53–75; see also Robert D. Marcus, *Grand Old Party: Political Structure in the Gilded Age* (New York, 1971); Horace S. Merrill, *Bourbon Democracy of the Middle West, 1865–1896* (Seattle, 1953); Paul Kleppner, *The Cross of Culture: A Social Analysis of Mid-western Politics, 1850–1900* (New York, 1970); and Kleppner, *The Third Electoral System* (Chapel Hill, 1979). For Nebraska politics from the 1880s onward, see Albert Watkins, *History of Nebraska* (Lincoln, 1913); Addison Erwin Sheldon, *Nebraska: The Land and the People*, 3 vols. (Chicago, 1931); James C. Olson, *J. Sterling Morton* (Lincoln, 1942); Frederick C. Luebke, *Immigrants and Politics: The Germans of Nebraska, 1880–1900* (Lincoln, 1969); Stanley Parsons, *The Populist Context: Rural versus Urban Power on a Great Plains Frontier* (Westport, 1973); and Robert W. Cherny, *Populism, Progressivism, and the Transformation of Nebraska Politics, 1885–1914* (Lincoln, 1981). For Lincoln, Nebraska, see Andrew J. Sawyer, ed., *Lincoln and Lancaster County Nebraska*, 2 vols. (Chicago, 1916).

On Populism, the best treatment is still John D. Hicks, *The Populist Revolt* (Minneapolis, 1931). See also John D. Barnhart, "The Farmers' Alliance and the People's Party in Nebraska" (Ph.D. dissertation, Harvard University, 1927). There are many other important sources for Populism, both nationally and in Nebraska; the bibliographies in the works by Parsons and Cherny contain the important sources for Nebraska. The most recent full-scale treatment of Populism is Lawrence Goodwyn, *Democratic Promise: The Populist Moment in America* (New York, 1976). Goodwyn views Populism as a counterculture, and calls Nebraska Populists a "shadow movement." For contrary views, see Robert W. Cherny, "Lawrence Goodwyn and Nebraska Populism: A Review Essay," *Great Plains Quarterly*, 1 (1981): 181–194, and Stanley B. Parsons et al., "The Role of Cooperatives in the Development of the Movement Culture of Populism," *Journal of American History*, 69 (1983): 866–885.

On Grover Cleveland, see Horace S. Merrill, *Bourbon Leader: Grover Cleveland and the Democratic Party* (Boston, 1957); and Allan Nevins, *Grover Cleveland: A Study in Courage* (New York, 1932). For the silver issue, see Allen Weinstein, *Prelude to Populism: Origins of the Silver Issue* (New Haven, 1970), and Paolo E. Coletta, "Greenbackers, Goldbugs, and Silverites: Currency Reform and Policy, 1860–1897," in *The Gilded Age: A Reappraisal,* edited by H. Wayne Morgan (Syracuse, 1963). The 1896 election has received a good deal of attention; see especially Stanley L. Jones, *The Presidential Election of 1896* (Madison, 1964); Paul W. Glad, *McKinley, Bryan and the People* (Philadelphia, 1964); William Diamond, "Urban and Rural Voting in 1896," *American Historical Review,* 46 (1941): 281–305; Richard Jensen, *The Winning of the Midwest: Social and Political Conflict, 1888–1896* (Chicago, 1971); and Kleppner and Luebke, cited above. For William McKinley, see H. Wayne Morgan, *William McKinley and His America* (Syracuse, 1963) and Lewis L. Gould, *The Presidency of William McKinley* (Lawrence, 1980).

For the Spanish-American War, see David F. Trask, *The War with Spain in 1898* (New York, 1981), and for imperialism see Ernest R. May, *Imperial Democracy: The Emergence of America as a Great Power* (New York, 1961). For Bryan's activities during the war, see J. R. Johnson, "William Jennings Bryan, The Soldier," *Nebraska History,* 31 (1950): 95–106. The anti-imperialist movement has generated a great deal of attention in the past few decades. Among the important treatments are: E. Berkeley Tompkins, *Anti-Imperialism in the United States* (Philadelphia, 1970); Daniel B. Shirmer, *Republic or Empire* (Cambridge, 1972); and Robert L. Beisner, *Twelve Against Empire* (New York, 1968). Older treatments include: Fred Harrington, "The Anti-Imperialist Movement in the United States, 1898–1900," *Mississippi Valley Historical Review,* 22 (1935): 211–230; and Maria C. Lanzar-Carpio, "The Anti-Imperialist League," *Philippine Social Science Review* 3 (1930): 7–41, 118–132; 4 (1931): 182–198, 239–254; 5, (1932): 222–230. For emphasis on the role of Populists and silverites, see Robert W. Cherny, "Anti-Imperialism on the Middle Border, 1898–1900," *Midwest Review,* 2nd series, 1 (1979): 19–34.

On the Chautauqua, see Charles F. Horner, *Strike the Tents: The Story of the Chautauqua* (Philadelphia, 1954), especially chapter 6; and John Bolton Bartlett, "Bryan, Chautauqua's Orator" (Ph.D. dissertation, Ohio State University, 1963). On Bryan's speaking, see also Boyce House, "Bryan the Orator," *Journal of the Illinois State Historical Society*, 53 (1960): 266–282.

The Progressive era has generated a large and complex historiography; for a good survey of recent writings, see Daniel T. Rodgers, "In Search of Progressivism," *Reviews in American History*, 10 (1982): 113–132. Richard L. McCormick, "The Discovery that 'Business Corrupts Politics': A Reappraisal of the Origins of Progressivism," *American Historical Review*, 86 (1981): 247–274, is essential. Recent works include John W. Chambers, *The Tyranny of Change* (New York, 1980); Arthur S. Link and Richard L. McCormick, *Progressivism* (Arlington Heights, 1983); and John Milton Cooper, Jr., *The Warrior and the Priest: Woodrow Wilson and Theodore Roosevelt* (Cambridge, 1983). For Bryan's role, see Paul W. Glad, "Bryan and the Urban Progressives," *Mid-America*, 39 (1957): 169–179; Edgar A. Hornig, "The Indefatigable Mr. Bryan in 1908," *Nebraska History*, 37 (1956): 183–200; Norbert R. Mahnken, "William Jennings Bryan in Oklahoma," *Nebraska History*, 31 (1950): 247–274. On the prohibition movement, begin with Peter H. Odegard, *Pressure Politics: The Story of the Anti-Saloon League* (New York, 1928). Other important works include: James H. Timberlake, *Prohibition and the Progressive Movement* (Cambridge, 1963); and Jack S. Blocker, Jr., *Retreat from Reform: The Prohibition Movement in the United States, 1890–1913* (Westport, 1976). For 1912, see Boyce House, "Bryan at Baltimore, the Democratic National Convention of 1912," *Nebraska History*, 41 (1960): 29–52; and Estal E. Sparlin, "Bryan and the 1912 Democratic Convention," *Mississippi Valley Historical Review*, 22 (1936): 537–546.

On Wilson, Arthur Link's multi-volume biography, *Wilson* (Princeton, 1947–1965),is standard; see also his *Woodrow Wilson: Revolution, War, and Peace* (Arlington Heights, Ill., 1979). For Bryan as Secretary of State, see Richard Challener, "William Jennings Bryan," in *An Uncertain Tradition: American Secretaries of State in the Twentieth Century*, ed. by Norman A. Graebner (New York, 1961); and Roger Daniels, "William Jennings Bryan and the Japanese," *Southern California Quarterly*, 48 (1966): 227–240. The Wilson's policy toward Latin America has produced many studies, notably Kenneth J. Grieb, *The United States and Huerta* (Lincoln, 1969); Peter Calvert, *The Mexican Revolution, 1910–1914: The Diplomacy of Anglo-American Conflict* (Cambridge,1968); Mark T. Gilderhus, *Diplomacy and Revolution: U.S.-Mexican Relations under Wilson and Carranza* (Tucson, 1977); and Friedrich Katz, *The Secret War in Mexico: Europe, the United States, and the Mexican Revolution* (Chicago, 1981).

The literature on the coming of war in 1914–1917 is extensive; see especially Ernest R. May, "Bryan and the World War, 1914–1915"(Ph.D. dissertation, U.C.L.A., 1951), and *The World War and American Isolation, 1914–1917* (Cambridge, 1959); May's views influenced my treatment of material in chapter 7. See also John Milton Cooper, Jr., *The Vanity of Power: American Isolationism and the First World War, 1914–1917* (Westport, 1969); Patrick Devlin, *Too Proud to Fight: Woodrow Wilson's Neutrality* (New York, 1975); C. Roland Marchand, *The American Peace Movement and Social Reform, 1898–1918* (Princeton, 1972); Daniel M. Smith, *Robert Lansing and American Neutrality: 1914–1917* (Berkeley and Los Angeles, 1958).

For the 1920s, start with Frederick Lewis Allen, *Only Yesterday* (New York, 1931); and William E. Leuchtenburg, *The Perils of Prosperity, 1914–1932* (Chicago, 1958). For the Ku Klux Klan and the election of 1924, look at David M. Chalmers, *Hooded Americanism* (New York, 1981); and Kenneth C. Mackay, *The Progressive Movement of 1924* (New York, 1947). On the Fundamentalist movement, see Louis Gaspar, *The Fundamentalist Movement* (The Hague,1963); Ernest R. Sandeen, *The Roots of Fundamentalism* (Chicago, 1970); George M. Marsden, *Fundamentalism and American Culture* (New York, 1980); and Willard B. Gatewood, Jr., ed., *Controversy in the Twenties* (Nashville, 1969). Ferenc Szasz, *The Divided Mind of Protestant America, 1880–1930* (University, Ala., 1982) is an important contribution to understanding the central role of Bryan in elevating evolution to a litmus of Fundamentalism.

The Scopes Trial generated a great deal of literature. Several versions of the transcript have appeared in print; the version by Leslie H. Allen, *Bryan and Darrow at Dayton* (New York, 1925; New York, 1967), contains some additional commentary. Treatments of the trial and the issues include: Ray Ginger, *Six Days or Forever?* (Boston, 1958); L. Sprague De Camp, *The Great Monkey Trial* (Garden City, 1968); Jerry R. Tompkins, *D-Days at Dayton* (Baton Rouge. 1965); and Frank W. C. Johnson, "A Rhetorical Criticism of the Speaking of William Jennings Bryan and Clarence Seward Darrow at the Scopes Trial" (Ph.D. dissertation, Western Reserve University, 1960).

Other doctoral dissertations, in addition to those already listed, include: Thomas Nagle, "An Historical Evaluation of William Jennings Bryan: His Public Career and Political Ideals, 1891–1915" (St. John's University, 1955); John Herbert Sloan, "William Jennings Bryan's Convention and Acceptance Speeches: 1896–1912" (University of Illinois, 1961); Marietta Stevenson, "William Jennings Bryan as a Political Leader" (University of Chicago, 1926); and Robert V. Supple, "The Political Rise of William Jennings Bryan from 1888 to the Nomination for the Presidency by the Democratic Party in 1896" (New York University, 1951). For masters' theses, see Frederick W. Adrian, *Theses and Dissertations Dealing with Nebraska and Nebraskans* (Lincoln, 1975).

Fairview, the Bryans' home from 1901 to 1921, has been restored and is maintained as a museum by the Nebraska State Historical Society. Bryan's birthplace in Salem is also maintained as a museum.

Copies of this manuscript, with references fully documented, and a full-length, partially annotated bibliography, have been deposited with the Nebraska State Historical Society, Lincoln, and Occidental College, Los Angeles.

Index

215